THE LIVERPOOL & MANCHESTER RAILWAY

ANTHONY DAWSON

AMBERLEY

Cover images courtesy of Ian Hardman Photography.

First published 2016

Amberley Publishing
The Hill, Stroud,
Gloucestershire, GL5 4EP

www.amberley-books.com

ISBN: 978 1 4456 6188 9 (print)
ISBN: 978 1 4456 6189 6 (ebook)

British Library Cataloguing in Publication Data.
A catalogue record for this book is available from the British Library.

Typeset in 10pt on 13pt Celeste.
Typesetting by Amberley Publishing.
Printed in the UK.

.

Contents

Acknowledgements

It is traditional at this point to thank those who have helped a book come to fruition: I would like to thank Paul Dore, Lauren Jaye Gradwell, Duncan Hough and Matthew Jackson for the use of personal photographs and Andy Mason for his support, numerous cups of tea and road trips along the Liverpool & Manchester. Also, to Judy Tuner for her proofreading.

I should also like to thank Will High (railway officer), Peter Brown, Richard Garside, Ian Hardman, Mike Ward, Lee Shaw and other railway volunteers at the Museum of Science and Industry Manchester who, against all odds, keep the spirit and traditions of

Railway volunteers past and present gathered at Liverpool Road on 5 January 2016 to mark the severing of the main-line connection and access to the 'Pineapple Line' by the controversial Ordsall Chord, bringing down the curtain on 185 years of railway operation. (Author)

the Liverpool & Manchester Railway alive; for their friendship, knowledge and technical hands-on skill. It is to all the railway volunteers, past and present, that this work is respectfully dedicated.

Photographs

All photographs, unless credited otherwise, are reproduced by the kind permission of the Museum of Science & Industry, Manchester.

INTRODUCTION

InterCity 185: The Liverpool & Manchester Railway 1830–2015

Opened on 15 September 1830, at a cost of £1,089,818 17s 7d, the Liverpool & Manchester was not the world's first public railway: that was the 'Lake Lock Railroad', which opened in 1796 in Yorkshire. Nor was it the first to use steam locomotives commercially – another Yorkshire 'first', the Middleton Railway in Leeds used locomotives successfully from 1812. It was, however, the first inter-city railway, and the first to use steam locomotives exclusively to carry passengers and goods throughout (the entrance to Liverpool notwithstanding). It was also the first double-track railway, the first to be fully timetabled, the first to carry mail and the first to carry soldiers on active duty (1832). It was also the first to issue printed regulations, which later influenced those of all the major British railway companies (other than the Great Western) and parliament in the regulation of railways.

The railway was the brainchild of the engineer William James and two wealthy industrialists, Joseph Sanders of Liverpool and John Kennedy of Manchester. The company was founded in 1823 by Henry Booth of Liverpool; Booth would later serve simultaneously as secretary and treasurer, and was also first secretary to the London & North Western Railway. Booth was also an inventor in his own right, suggesting to Robert Stephenson the multi-tubular boiler as well as inventing a form of axle grease and sprung draw and buffing gear for the rolling stock.

It had a troubled gestation; the first Act (1825) was thrown out, largely as a result of the errors in the survey carried out by George Stephenson, and his subsequent poor performance before a parliamentary committee. With Stephenson discredited, the directors then appointed John and George Rennie as their engineers and Charles Blacker Vignoles as surveyor. A second survey on an alternative route, one which avoided the property of several peers who were opposed to the railway, was made. The Enabling Act was ably steered through parliament with aid of William Huskisson, MP for Liverpool and president of the Board of Trade, receiving Royal Assent in 1826. Stephenson, however, was reappointed as chief engineer after the departure of Vignoles, and subsequently the Rennies, as they were unable to work with the heavy-handed Stephenson. Joseph Locke was appointed as his assistant. Third and fourth Acts were required to divert the railway into Manchester and to cross the River Irwell in 1829. It was absorbed by the Grand Junction Railway in 1845 and, in 1846, became part of the L&NWR.

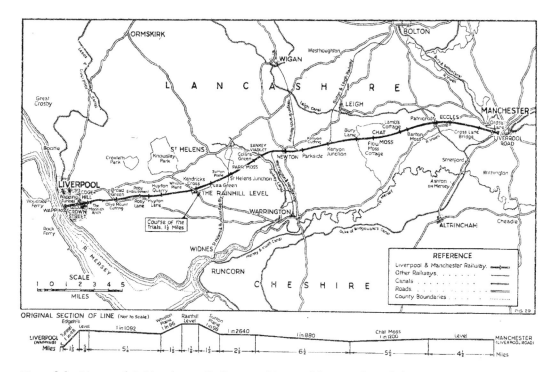

Map of the Liverpool & Manchester Railway and its neighbouring branch lines.

CHAPTER 1

Liverpool Road, Manchester

The location of the Manchester terminus of the Liverpool & Manchester was the subject of controversy: George Stephenson in 1825 had originally proposed to enter Manchester from the south-west to a terminus on Quay Street, as 'collectively this area represented the greatest concentration of warehousing in Manchester'. However, Ann Atherton and her sister Eleanora Byrom played a major role in blocking the passage of the railway through Manchester, as they claimed it would ruin property prices. Mrs Atherton's late husband, Henry, had been busy laying out the area between Liverpool Road and Charles Street as a genteel middle-class urban development. Opposition also came from the Old Quay Company, who had a monopoly on waterborne transport and warehousing in the city.

In 1826, therefore, Charles Vignoles decided to avoid entering Manchester altogether, and thus also avoid the expense of bridging the River Irwell, terminating his line alongside the New Bailey Prison in Salford. This was the route approved by the Liverpool & Manchester Railway Act (5 May 1826) and, in the following year, Stephenson found himself again in sole charge of the engineering of the railway. It was suggested to the Railway Company that they purchase 6,000 square yards of land opposite Liverpool Road that was occupied by the dyeworks of Rothwell & Harrison (they continued as tenants of the railway company) on which to build their new terminus; additional land was purchased bounded by Charles Street, Water Street and Liverpool Road from one Gilbert Winter. Finally, the recently built (c. 1820) house on the corner of Liverpool Road and Water Street was purchased from Mrs Atherton and Miss Byrom – this was to become the station agent's house. This deviation to the original route (and the crossing of the Irwell) received Royal Assent on 14 May 1829.

The Athertons and Byroms, however, were not finished yet: the Railway Company was bound by an agreement made with the Byroms that locomotives were not to be used over any of the lands formerly owned by Edward Byrom without the written consent of his daughter, Eleanora. More serious, however, was the opposition from the local government of Manchester. They insisted that locomotives could only be used with the consent of the surveyors of highways and the police commissioners, except on the Railway Company's own property and over the Water Street Bridge. Any breach would lead to a £20 fine.

The Passenger Station

The surviving Liverpool Road station buildings were built in phases over several years. The original block consisted of the first- and second-class booking offices and waiting rooms. It was built by David Bellhouse, who had also won the contract to build the warehouse opposite. The *Manchester Mercury* (22 June 1830) states:

> Workmen are now employed in digging the foundations for a handsome and extensive coach office, eighty feet in length, to be erected immediately adjoining the house lately occupied by Mr Rothwell. The coach office will consist of three stories, two of which will be below the level of the railway and the third above it. The western front of this building will look into Liverpool Road along which it will extend: and the other front (consisting of one storey) will look upon the railway exactly opposite the warehouses now erecting. In this part of the building, the principal office will be situated. The erection will consist, in a considerable degree, if not principally of stone, and the remainder will be covered with a coating of Roman Cement so that its appearance will be highly ornamental.

A month later the building had reached second-floor level and it is safe to assume that by the opening day (15 September 1830) it was largely complete. John Scott Walker, writing in 1830, describes the building as 'a spacious building with a Grecian front to Liverpool Road.

Liverpool Road station as it probably appeared on opening day in 1830. (Author's Collection)

This will be the Station for the reception of passengers who will pass immediately through the building to and from the carriages ... '

Passengers entered at street level from Liverpool Road: first-class passengers entered through the grand main entrance, flanked by paired pilasters topped with a curious carved urn. After 1833 a sundial was affixed over the first-class entrance. Second-class passengers entered through a similar, though less grand entrance – which rather mars the symmetry of the building. First- and second-class booking halls and waiting rooms were not linked; admission to the waiting rooms situated directly above the two booking halls was via a broad wooden staircases (the second class was subsequently removed) and were for ticket-holders only.

Liverpool Road station, with the class system written large in stone. The first-class entrance and waiting room has the imposing entrance flanked by pilasters echoed in the window above; then, the more domestic-looking second-class entrance; and the goods office. (Author)

Interior of the spacious first-class booking hall, where tickets had to be purchased 24 hours before departure time.

The broad, curving staircase linking the first-class booking hall with its equally spacious waiting room above.

Tickets, Please

Purchasing tickets was a convoluted process: they had to be bought 24 hours in advance of the desired travel time and the potential passenger had to leave details of next of kin, their name, age, address and why they wished to travel. Passengers had to travel on the specified train and the company did not hold itself responsible if luggage was damaged in transit. Passengers were also forbidden to drink and smoke. Lines of differing lengths were printed on the back of the tickets to inform illiterate ticket inspectors how far the passenger wished to travel. The Liverpool & Manchester, like the Stagecoach companies before them, operated on a 'waybill system':

> ... at the booking office ... our tickets, which will be found to be numbered to correspond with the seats allotted to us in the carriages, we proceed up a flight of stairs and find ourselves in a spacious apartment used by passengers in waiting for any of the trains. It is commodiously fitted up for comfort and convenience ...

In other words, passengers had to travel in their booked seat, in their booked carriage and in the correct train: only a 50 per cent refund could be claimed. Before the train started, the guard would hand to the engineman a slip bearing the names of himself, his fireman, the guards as well as the composition and weight of the train, and the starting time. Any special instructions for setting-down passengers on a second-class train were also included.

A first-class fare in 1830 cost 7s, (compared to 10s for a stagecoach, which could take up to 8 hours), which was a non-stop journey from either end of the line, only pausing to take on water at Parkside. The journey was timed to take 90 minutes. A second-class fare cost 4s and took 2 hours, the train stopping at the intermediate stations. Third class was only

Timetable and booking information from March 1831, with handwritten amendments. (Author's collection)

introduced on the Liverpool & Manchester in 1844 (and only because parliament said they had to), during the last year of company's existence, using the former second-class 'Blue Coaches', at 2s 6d. From 1830, trains were timetabled to depart ten times a day, which was increased to twelve the following year, leaving Liverpool and Manchester at the same time:

6.00 a.m. (summer)	2.00 p.m. (first class)
7.00 a.m. (first class)	3.00 p.m.
7.15 a.m.	4.00 p.m. (summer)
9.00 a.m.	5.00 p.m. (first class)
10.00 a.m.	5.30 p.m.
12.00 noon	7.00 p.m.

The first public passenger train, and indeed first charter train, was run on 16 September 1830, when 150 members of the Religious Society of Friends (Quakers) chartered a train from Liverpool to Manchester to attend a quarterly meeting. The journey took 90 minutes at a cost of 7s. Full-time operation did not commence until the following day (17 September): between 17 and 25 September, some 6,104 passengers (or 763 per day) were carried, far outstripping expectations. Trains were run on Sunday, but not during the hours of divine worship, with two trains (one first, one second) each way. The timetable of March 1831 lists a second-class train using the enclosed coaches, presumably for first-class passengers who lived between each terminal city. 'Mixed' or 'merchant's' trains of first- and second-class carriages were run from 1836, departing each end of the line at 7 p.m., stopping only at Newton. There was also an option of 'extra first class' travelling in the mail coach, and, for

The rail side of the station buildings, viewed from the footplate of *Planet*. The first-class entrance is on the right, second-class on the left. Passengers would have been extremely cramped and, until a 'landing stage' was built, had to climb into their carriages. Next to the clock is the bracket for the original station bell, rung 5 minutes before departure time.

the wealthiest passengers, there was always the option of travelling in their own private road carriage, carried on a specially designed carriage truck. With the opening of the North Union (1834) and Grand Junction (1837), Henry Booth reported that in 1841 up to six trains an hour were arriving at Manchester.

Contrasting with the comfort of the waiting rooms, the area used by passengers at rail level was very small – it would have been a crowded, bustling place, especially given that, at this point, the railway was four tracks wide, with goods wagons as well as departing and arriving passenger trains (and their passengers). There was no platform and passengers had to climb physically into their carriages until 1833, when a 'landing stage' was erected. Nor was there any protection from the elements until 1834, when a canopy was provided. A large bell was rung 5 minutes before departure time to warn passengers to board their trains.

The Station Grows

The office accommodation at Liverpool Road was almost immediately found to be insufficient, so an eastward extension was added: the foundations 'of the carrier's office' were being laid in July 1830. The main entrance to this new block was almost identical in design to the second-class entrance, but to a simpler design: the class system writ large in brick and stone. Two ground-floor rooms acted as a parcels office, which communicated via the second-class staircase to rail level. The first-floor level was originally a screen with nothing behind. By 1837 the carrier's office had become the booking office and waiting room for the Grand Junction Railway; by around 1840 a second storey had been added to create waiting accommodation. A spare office was used from 1834 as a booking office for onward journeys to Chester and other places: the journey could begin by train and then be completed by stagecoach. In this way through tickets to places like Southport were developed.

A further eastward extension took place during 1830–31 when a range of 'several handsome shops' was erected, extending the range of buildings to some 500 feet. One of the first tenants (July 1831) was one William Vickers, who was paying an annual rent of £35 on the premises for his coffee shop. In addition, there was also a beer shop, both no doubt catering to railway travellers and workers. The Railway Company in fact licensed the beer shop in 1843 as a public house. The first floor level was merely a screen – above the row of shops was a two-track carriage shed designed to hold twenty carriages. With the cessation of passenger-carrying at Liverpool Road (4 May 1844), the shops were converted into workshops and the open side of the carriage shed was bricked up to become stores; the station, however, appears to have been used by third-class passengers – during the Whitsun

The extensive range of buildings on Liverpool Road, completed between 1830 and 1832. The station agent's house is just visible on the corner of Water Street; lurking behind is the bulk of the 1830 Warehouse. (Author)

Liverpool Road, 1962. Note the signal box, which was demolished during the restoration of the site, and the numerous telegraph poles. (Author's Collection)

holidays of 1846, some 5,355 passengers travelled third-class to Liverpool and back: 'for a double ticket ... half a crown.'

In order to cater for railway passengers, Benjamin Taylor opened the Railway & Commercial Inn on Liverpool Road, advertising in September 1830 that:

> He has OPENED a NEW and COMMODIOUS INN, immediately opposite the Company's Offices, where BREAKFASTS, DINNERS &c. are regularly provided for the accommodation of such Passengers, at times suitable for the arrival and departure of the conveyances.

By 1837 it was known as the 'Railway and Commercial Hotel' and was still advertising 'Breakfasts, Chops, Steaks, or Dinners on the shortest notice' to railway passengers, as well assuring them of 'Good Stabling with Lock-ups and Coach Houses'. Despite early success,

The open-sided, two-road carriage shed, built in 1831 to store twenty carriages. After closure to passengers in the 1840s, the carriage shed became the rope and sheet repair shops, repairing the tarpaulins for railway goods wagons and carts.

The Railway & Commercial Inn, on Liverpool Road, opened in 1830 offering accommodation, stabling and meals for rail travellers. (Author)

the whole property – including furniture, cutlery and even the staircases – was put up for auction in 1843, and again ten years later.

Due to the somewhat out of the way location of the station, an omnibus was run from the company's coach office at 57 Market Street (the junction with Market Street and New Cannon Street – now somewhere under the Arndale Shopping Mall). There were four 'Buses, for first class passengers only, each painted dark green with gilt letters bearing the name "Auxillium"'. Operated by Henry Charles Lacy of Manchester, they were 'well built and commodious glass coaches to hold sixteen inside and two on the box beside the driver, and luggage on the roof with oil cloth to keep the same dry'. They ran on three routes, picking up and setting down passengers:

> Liverpool Road – Water Street – Quay Street – Deansgate – St Mary's Gate – Market Street.
> Liverpool Road – Water Street – Bridge Street – Deansgate – King Street – Pall Mall – Market Street.
> Liverpool Road – Bridgwater Street – Mosley Street – Market Street.

Lacy also designed and had built a rather unusual vehicle, which allowed a road carriage to be conveyed by the railway, described by the *Manchester Mercury*:

> This vehicle has been constructed so that it may be drawn upon its own wheels from the residence of any Gentleman to the railway, and the body of the carriage may then be raised from the wheels by means of a crane and placed upon a frame or wagon having wheels adapted for the railway. It is then conveyed along the line and at the end of the journey may be replaced upon a set of ordinary wheels and driven along the streets to the final destination of the passenger or family, for whose exclusive use it may be devoted … It is elegantly fitted up and is capable of containing six individuals inside and two in front … The present carriage has been ordered merely by way of Experiment and it is not yet certain whether this novel mode of conveyance will be finally adopted.

Goods & Warehouses

The Liverpool Road Railway Warehouse is the world's first railway warehouse – and the world's oldest. It was based upon pre-existing design features for canal warehouses: railway wagons entered the building at rail level, after having been turned through 90 degrees using turntables, and were then unloaded. The building is curved, five bays long, with an extreme length of 320 feet and a depth of 70 feet. Each of the bays was used to store different goods: butter, grocery, spirits and corn (two bays). The floor levels comprised a cellar (including a 50-foot-deep well), a ground floor at street level, rail level and top storey. In 1831 an intermediate floor was added between the ground floor and rail level.

These warehouses were designed to hold 10,000 bales of cotton 'or other merchandise in proportion'. Tenders were let on 27 March 1830; five firms submitted estimates, with David Bellhouse Jnr eventually gaining the contract for £12,683, on the understanding that two of

This view of 1830 Warehouse from the lower yard emphasises the scale of the building and of the Liverpool Road site.

the warehouses (bays) were to be finished by July 1830 and the remainder by August 1830. The *Manchester Mercury* noted on 15 June 1830 that,

> The extensive range of warehouses is within few feet of the full height to which it is intended to be carried, the fourth storey from the ground being nearly erected.

However, due to the pressure imposed by the directors on Bellhouse, his workmen went on strike:

> The erection ... has been somewhat impeded by a turn-out of the labourers for an advance of wages, which was succeeded by a turn-out of the brick-setters. Mr Bellhouse ... who is bound by contract to have them completed by the end of July, under a heavy penalty, found it necessary to comply with the demands of both classes of workmen; and the time which was lost during the turn-out has since been made-up by working over hours.

The *Manchester Mercury* also noted a last-minute change of design to the station: instead of the line 'carrying on as far as the warehouses extended', twelve additional arches were built to carry the line 'to the top of the field in which it terminates'. The *Manchester Guardian* reported on 24 July 1830 that the warehouses had been roofed and were nearing completion. The building was probably complete by opening day: the upper storey was used for the cold collation for 1,000 persons on the opening day (15 September 1830), supplied by Mr Lymm of the Waterloo Hotel, Manchester. A temporary staircase was erected on the outside of the building to give access to the upper storeys. In the end, the opening festivities were marred by William Huskisson's fatal accident and the hostile mob that awaited the Duke of Wellington. And, with it being Manchester, of course it rained.

The internal lifting gear was mechanised in 1830 under the superintendence of George Stephenson and a steam engine was supplied for £340 by Thompson, Swift & Cole of Bolton in 1831. The engine house was built against the western (Water Street) end of the building with a tall chimney to disperse the smoke. All the machinery on the site was subsequently replaced by hydraulic machinery in the late nineteenth century; a hydraulic tower was built on the corner of Lower Byrom Street and Grape Street and the original accumulator house was in Water Street.

The relationship between the various buildings and the size of the 320-foot-long 1830 Warehouse is clearly demonstrated in this view of the lower yard. Just visible on the left – at rail level – are the passenger station building as well the underpass from the lower yard through to Liverpool Road.

The imposing mass of the 1830 Warehouse, as seen from rail level.

The Shipping Shed

The single warehouse was unable to cope with the rapid development of freight traffic on the site. Only a year after opening, Franklin & Haigh of Liverpool were requested to prepare designs for a new shipping shed, to be erected on the south-eastern corner of the site, running parallel with Liverpool Road. The shipping shed was described in 1839 as

> ... a loading-warehouse, with proper wharf and cranes, and an inclined road up from Liverpool Road. The building is about 225 feet in length along the Liverpool Road, and 42 feet in width. The front is next to the railway, which is here laid with three sets of rails; besides one line which runs within and along the whole length of the building.

The new building appears to have been largely built of timber; in 1836 the boarded side of the shipping shed along Liverpool Road was replaced with brickwork. This building was replaced in around 1855 (tenders were advertised in January 1855) by a much larger brick-built structure (now known as the 'Powerhall'), built on newly acquired land on the corner of what is now Lower Byrom Street and Liverpool Road. The *Manchester Times* (11 October 1854) records that, 'Preparations are now being made to connect the goods railway in Liverpool Road, with the proposed vegetable market' on Knott Mill (a.k.a. Campfield) fairground on Liverpool Road and now occupied by the 'Air and Space Hall' (itself a market hall built in 1876). Houses in Wellington Place (now part of Lower Byrom

Exterior of the 1855 Shipping Shed, replacing the earlier structure of 1831, and built on the site of back-to-back slum dwellings known as 'Wellington Place'. The main vehicular access was on the corner of Liverpool Road and Lower Byrom Street.

Street) had been pulled down to allow the extension of the station site. The land was compulsorily purchased by Manchester Corporation, who wanted the railway to extend to its proposed Market Hall. In 1857, the Railway Company reneged on its deal with the Corporation and was forced to pay back £2,000.

In the north side of the shipping shed were two running roads; down the centre was a timber platform and loading dock, so that goods could be quickly and efficiently transferred from rail to road. Road access was on the south side. The new facilities at Liverpool Road were probably inspired by the opening of the Birkenhead, Lancashire & Cheshire Junction Railway (1850), who advertised they were shipping goods from Liverpool Road in November 1853. The BL&CJR became the 'Birkenhead Railway' in 1859 and next year a London & North Western Railway (LNWR) and Great Western (GWR) joint line, giving the GWR a foothold in Manchester. During 1860 the LNWR spent £1,374 on 'cranes and steam machinery' at Liverpool Road. Outside the shipping shed in later years was a two-road overhead iron gantry crane, fitted with two moveable electric cranes with a 60-ton lifting capacity. In July 1866, two porters – Thomas Brewer and George Cranshaw – were injured when 'one of the large doors [of the shipping shed] fell upon them'.

Running perpendicularly from the shipping shed was the coal dock, some 200 feet long and incorporating two coal-drops where 'common road wagons are loaded from the railway by means of ... coal-shoots'. Contiguous to the coal yard was a timber yard. James Fitton took over the coal yard in summer 1834, supplying 'Wigan house coal' at 10s 10d per ton.

The upper yard, showing on the right the 1855 shipping shed (now known as the 'Power Hall') and the overhead crane gantry, with its twin electric cranes, built around 1890. In the background is the roof of the 'Air and Space Hall', built in 1876 as a market hall. By the 1920s, the shipping shed had become known as the 'Old Shed'.

The *c.* 1860 goods inquiry office, built in typical LNWR style, adjoining the shipping shed built a few years previously.

Additional Warehouses

A further two ranges of cotton warehouses were erected in 1831 to store 10,000 bales of cotton. Five Manchester firms tendered, the contract being let to Samuel Buxton (£13,885). According to Francis Wishaw in 1839, No. 1 Warehouse measured 200 feet by 70 feet, parallel to the 1830 warehouse, while the second, No. 2 Warehouse, at right angles, measured 200 feet by 90 feet. Wishaw estimated the 'area of warehouse room in the several floors at five acres and the warehousing capacity at upwards of four millions of cubic feet'. He went on to say:

> One of the floors of both the first [1830 Warehouse] and third stacks [No. 2 Warehouse], which are level with the railway, are laid cross lines of way, so that the wagons, by means of turn-tables, are conveyed and loaded, or unloaded, within the warehouse; and by loop-holes next the warehouse-streets, and flaps in the floors, the arrangement for quick despatch of business ... are rendered exceedingly complete.
>
> There are bridge-ways from the first [1830 Warehouse] to the second [No. 1 Warehouse which ran parallel], and from the second to the third [No. 2 Warehouse] on the level of the railway... The chief entrance for road-wagons to the warehouses is in Water Street ... and there is a way out under the railway into the Liverpool Road.

The 1830 Warehouse and No. 1 Warehouse were linked by an overhead tramway, which was linked to No. 2 Warehouse by 1839. The Grand Junction had its own warehouse on the site, opened in 1837. Not all customers remembered to collect their goods: Messrs Capes & Smith of Manchester sold on the behalf of the LNWR on 6 April 1848 'a considerable quantity of valuable goods', which had not been collected from the warehouses, including

6 tons of logwood (a dyeing agent), twenty-eight casks of cement, twenty-one barrels of rosin, thirty sacks of guano, ten sacks of rice flour and six woollen shawls that had been left in the carriages.

Above: Through this central opening at rail level on the south side, tracks directly entered the 1830 Warehouse and exited via the north side, connecting to No. 1 Warehouse via an overhead tramway. Each of the five bays of the 1830 Warehouse was accessed from rail level through large, arched doorways. In front of each was a wagon turntable so that vehicles could be turned through 90 degrees and run directly into the building, copying canal warehouse practice.

Right: The north side of the 1830 Warehouse, showing where the overhead tramway exited, linking it with No. 1 Warehouse, which was destroyed by fire in 1866.

The Great Fire

A fire on 22 May 1866 destroyed No. 1 Warehouse, which had been used to store 'cotton, madder root, jute, and dye stuffs ... of the most inflammable nature'. The fire began in No. 2 Warehouse, which was being used to store chemicals and which was so badly damaged as to be 'beyond redemption'. Also threatened were No. 3 Warehouse (the 1830 warehouse: the heat was so intense that the doors and other woodwork started to burn) and the shipping shed, which was then being used to store 'butter, lard, tallow, sugar, flour' and 'great apprehensions were felt for some time' for the safety of the building. The fire was so massive as to require both the Manchester & Salford and the Ashton-under-Lyne fire brigades, but their efforts were 'puny' in extinguishing the blaze. The Broughton & Pendleton volunteers pulled down part of the 'tramway bridge connecting No. 3 warehouse' to No. 1, which no doubt saved that building. No. 1 Warehouse collapsed around 7.30 p.m., crushing Manchester fireman Henry Clarke. By midnight, there was nothing left of No. 1 Warehouse other than 'a smoking pile of ruins'. The damage was estimated to be £300,000. Some of the damaged goods were sold on: John Thomas of Manchester advertised 'Upwards of 500 sacks of Flour, slightly damaged by water' for sale at Liverpool Road, 30 May 1866. Messrs Harpin & Bower advertised rescued dye materials for sale the following month.

Redevelopment

The LNWR immediately set about rebuilding the site under the auspices of the L&NWR New Works and Additional Powers Act 1866, which also included new bridges over the Irwell and Water Street and widening the embankment between Ordsall Lane and Liverpool Road stations. Tenders were advertised in September 1866 for additional 'Bridges and Arching' at Liverpool Road and, in October 1866, they advertised tenders for 'The Erection of a Goods Warehouse at the Liverpool Road Station'. This was the fireproof, iron-framed, 'Bonded Goods Warehouse' (running parallel to Grape Street) and its viaduct; this was completed by 1869 and in operation by 1874.

The c. 1869 iron-framed, fire-proof Bonded Goods Warehouse on Grape Street, built in typical LNWR style.

In order to expand the site, the LNWR attempted to gain powers to purchase additional land 'lying on the north and east sides and adjoining the Liverpool Road station, and on the north side of Wellington Place ... adjoining Lower Byrom Street ... [and] Charles Street [present-day Grape Street]' in 1866 and 1872, with permission finally being granted in 1878. The court of directors of the LNWR voted some £118,000 for the 'enlargements of Liverpool-road Goods station' in 1876. On this land, in April 1880, the LNWR advertised tenders for 'the erection of a Goods Warehouse at Liverpool Road Station, Manchester'. This was the four-storey warehouse, which became known as the 'Great Western Warehouse' due to that company having exclusive use of a goods yard immediately to its north. The GWR yard was in existence by 1859, when John Paterson was the GWR's goods officer at Liverpool Road with an office on Charles Street. The GWR and Bonded Warehouses are connected via an impressive iron viaduct across the lower yard, completed by 1869.

The 1880s Great Western Warehouse, again in typical LNWR red and blue brick, built on the site of former back-to-back properties on the corner of Charles and Lower Byrom Street.

The upper yard from rail level, showing the relationship of the 1880s Great Western Warehouse, the overhead crane, and shipping shed. The two-road rail entrance of the latter is just visible on the right.

The lower yard, as seen from the upper yard, showing the relationship between the 1830 Warehouse and the iron viaduct, supported on elegant cast-iron Doric columns, which complimented the earlier Water Street Bridge of 1830.

The curved iron viaduct, linking the Bonded Warehouse (completed c. 1869) over the lower yard and across Water Street. It was built 1866–1869 on the site of the former No. 1 Warehouse, which was destroyed by fire. It became known as the 'Pineapple Line', due to the public house of that name on Water Street, which it ran past.

The 'Bonded Goods Warehouse' on Grape Street was effectively a customs warehouse (a customs officer was based there), which was used to store imported goods such as tea, spirits, or tobacco, without the payment of customs duty – although a 'customs bond' had to be lodged with the government. The top floor of the GWR Warehouse was also used to store bonded goods. By the 1870s the amount of cotton imported into Manchester had dropped to the extent that only one floor of the Bonded Warehouse was used to store it, the other floors being used to store tea, coffee, tobacco, perfume, but primarily wine and spirits. Liverpool Road became mainly concerned with perishable and consumable goods; the GWR Warehouse was used to store grain, flour, and general goods.

In the late nineteenth century, over 100 men and several hundred horses were employed at Liverpool Road. In 1938 Liverpool Road handled 246.5 million tons of freight; a decade later this had risen to 273 million tons. It was busier than ever before but, by the 1960s, the buildings had become dilapidated and the site was increasingly run down. It was closed by British Railways on 8 September 1975 and, unlike the grand opening in 1830, attracted no publicity whatsoever.

Goods returns to Liverpool Road: *Agecroft No. 1* (Robert Stephenson & Hawthorn, 1948), pulling a demonstration freight train. *Agecroft* was restored by volunteers at the museum between 2009 and 2011 at a cost of £120,000. (Duncan Hough)

LNWR wagons like this one would have been a common sight at Liverpool Road; in 1912, there were 311 horses working at the station, owned by the LNWR/LMS, GWR (who had stables on Deansgate) and the LNER (stables under railway arches on Bridgewater Street). On May Day, 'it was our treat to watch the GWR's shire horses ... all decked up for the parade ... their horses were always beautifully kept, not like those on the LNER'. (Author's Collection)

CHAPTER 2

Rails around Manchester

All Aboard!

The bell having been rung, it was time to board the train. Carriages on the Liverpool & Manchester were designed by a Quaker father-and-son team: Thomas Clarke and Nathaniel Worsdell of Liverpool. Nathaniel's eldest son, Thomas William, became locomotive superintendent of the Great Eastern Railway and thence the North Eastern, where he was succeeded by his younger brother, Wilson.

Both first- and second-class carriages shared a common underframe 16 feet long; the bodies being 15 feet, 6 inches long. Wheels were sprung and were 3 feet in diameter originally with a 7-foot wheelbase, which gave a rather pronounced 'see-saw' motion, especially when starting and stopping. Both types of carriage had three compartments: first-class seating six, three abreast (eighteen passengers in total), while second-class sat eight, four abreast (twenty-four passengers in total). In first-class carriages, the luggage (up to 60 lbs per passenger) was carried on the roof, while in second-class it was stored under the seats.

A first-class coach, as depicted by Isaac Shaw in 1831. In full stagecoach tradition, each of the first-class coaches were individually named; a list of twenty names has been reconstructed. Luggage was carried on the roof – at the owner's risk, of course. (Author's Collection)

A second-class (or 'blue') coach; in the 1830s, a second-class train was a stopping train (all stations), while first class was direct, with only a single stop at Parkside to take water. Before the introduction of roofs in 1833, the only concession to the weather was holes drilled in the floor to allow rainwater to escape. (Author's Collection)

Second-class carriages were 'panelled up to the elbow' and until 1831 lacked any roof or protection from the elements: the only concession to rain being holes drilled in the floor for drainage. By 1842 Henry Booth reported that the second-class carriages had their open ends 'boarded up', creating semi-open vehicles. One passenger in 1832 referred to them as 'travelling pneumonia wagons'. Another irate passenger thought that with roofs they were

Incomparably worse than if they had been open without a roof, that covering occasions such cutting currents of wind – I have not experienced rain – that the suffering is intense. They are no doubt constructed to increase the profits of the Company, by inducing the travellers to pay the first class fares. But is it not cruel – is it not unprincipled – is it not a mockery of limited means – to offer to convey persons for a smaller fare, only in such a manner that their health, and even their lives, are placed under great risk?

Following the introduction of new, enclosed, second-class carriages by the Grand Junction and the North Union Railways in 1837, a furious *Manchester Times* opined that:

The second class carriages ... seem to have been made as uncomfortable and unsightly as possible ... they are little better than those which are provided for the pigs ... either in point of comfort or decoration. It is true that they have a covering, but it only serves to concentre the current of cold air and makes it doubly injurious to health ... It is a paltry economy which they have been practicing.

First-class coaches were fully enclosed and were essentially three stagecoach bodies joined together on a common underframe. The *Liverpool Times* described the first-class coaches in glowing terms:

They give us quite a new idea of the ease and luxury with which persons may in future travel ... [they] consist, like the French diligences, of two or three bodies joined together ... The seats which accommodate three persons each are at least twice as wide as a four-inside stage-coach, so as to allow the same space for three as is now allotted to four. Between the

Exterior of a 1930-built replica first-class coach, named after William Huskisson MP. The primrose-yellow paint scheme, chosen by George Stephenson, replicated that of the fastest stage coaches. (Lauren Jaye Gradwell, 2016)

Interior of the replica first-class coach, which sat six persons almost knee to knee: 'upholstered in French grey cloth with buttons and lace to match ... the upholstery is carried to a considerable height above the seats, padded head rests being included'. (Lauren Jaye Gradwell, 2016)

sittings is a rest for the arms, and each passenger has a cushion for himself; and there is also a little projection against which he may rest his head; and the backs are padded and covered with fine cloth ... There is abundant space left for the legs.

Despite this high praise, having ridden in an original Manchester & Birmingham first-class carriage (c. 1840), the experience can only be described as claustrophobic, especially in the dark. The carriages were approximately 5 feet high internally with doors measuring 4 feet, 6 inches – the passenger was unable to stand and, rather like a modern car, railway carriages in the 1830s were something you sat down in. There is very little room from knee-to-knee (the compartments measure 6 feet wide by 5 feet long), and the somewhat cosy atmosphere would have been enhanced by ladies wearing voluminous dresses. The carriages were devoid of lighting until 1834 when two gas lamps were fitted, each lamp lighting half a compartment:

There are three divisions in the carriages ... the first lamp is fixed in the partition, so as to light the first and second apartment; the other one half in the third apartment, and the

Original 'Manchester & Birmingham Railway' first-class coach, c. 1840. Broadly similar to the Liverpool & Manchester examples.

other to the outside of the carriage, which lights the guard or brakesman, so that two gas lights do the purpose of four distinct lights.

The lamps gave 'sufficient light to enable any person to read the smallest print' and had been installed at the suggestion of one of the directors, D. Hodgson Esq., and fitted-up by Mr Taylor of the Manchester Gas Works. First- and second-class carriages lacked any buffing gear when new; Henry Booth in 1832 designed sprung buffers and sprung draw-gear, which from 1833 onwards was fitted to the first-class coaches. In order to ease the ride, new 'revolving carriage [axle] boxes' were fitted during 1832, the invention of a Mr Birch, consisting of 'a cylinder, divided (or, rather, two cylinders, with a ring between them), placed between the axle and the box of the wheel, which latter is provided with a chamber on the inside, and a concave screw cap on the outside, as reservoirs to contain oil'. A new axle grease developed by Henry Booth was in use from 1835. In the same year, the patent buffing gear, designed by T. F. Bergin of the Dublin & Kingstown Railway, was introduced. Henry Booth 'produced a new plan of applying the buffers', patented in 1836, which, together with his three-link screw coupling, was fitted to all of the carriages.

Six replica coaches were built at Derby by the LMS for the 1930 Railway Centenary: three first-class and three second-class. It is easy to see why some passengers referred to the second-class coaches as 'travelling pneumonia wagons', in comparison to the fully enclosed first-class vehicles. (Duncan Hough)

The precarious position of the guard, perched on the coach roof, is readily demonstrated: it is easy to see how they could freeze to death on a cold winter's night. (Matthew Jackson)

Guards

Seated on top of the coaches were the guards; the 'under guard' sat at the front of the train, facing backwards, and the 'upper guard' sat at the rear, facing forward. The 'upper guard' was in charge of the train and responsible for its safety; they were to ensure all the luggage was correctly stowed and the carriages were correctly coupled. The locomotive crew were to communicate with the guards – who each had control of the brake on the carriage upon which they sat – via the steam whistle: three short blasts ordered them to put the brakes on; three long to take them off. The guards communicated with each other via hand signals and coloured flags. Each guard was also issued with a red signal flag (stop; danger) and a triple-aspect hand lamp, which could show white (all clear), green (caution) and red (danger) 'at will'. Guards were also to collect money for tickets sold along the route and for this reason carried a heavy leather cash bag. It could be a cold, lonely job, especially for the guards on goods trains: William Tewburn, a goods guard, was killed at Liverpool Road, when he was run over by a train after falling from his precarious perch, his 'body benumbed by long exposure to cold'.

Out on the Road

The passengers having taken their seats, the porters, superintended by the guards, check that luggage is properly secured to the roofs of the carriages. This done, the signal to the guard that the train is safe to depart; the guard gives the 'Right Away' by blowing on his bugle, to which the fireman responds with his own: the steam whistle was not yet invented (c.1836). The engineman ensures *Planet* is in forward gear (foot pedal down – the foot pedal controls a pair of driving dogs (dog clutch) on the driving axle, which can be moved from left to right to engage forward or reverse gear); pushes forward the left-hand valve lever, pulls back the right-hand, and then opens *Planet*'s regulator, letting steam into her cylinders, slowly rolling forward. He grabs the left-hand lever and pulls it back, then quickly pushes the right-hand lever forward, manually operating the valves. He then repeats the process, left lever forward and right lever backward as *Planet* gently rolls away, making a distinct 'chuff' as each valve lever is operated. As *Planet* gets moving, he can lock the valves in place as she slowly picks up speed. The enginemen were strictly enjoined to 'start and stop their engines slowly and without a jerk, so as to avoid the risk of snapping the couplings'. The fireman was to look out and check that all the carriages were 'attached and all right'. The injunction to start slowly without a jerk was all the more important before the passenger carriages were fitted with effective buffing gear. One traveller in 1836 wrote how:

> At the instant of starting, the automaton [Engine] belches forth an explosion of steam, and seems, for a second or two, quiescent. But quickly the explosions are reiterated, with shorter and shorter intervals, till they become too rapid to be counted, though still distinct. These belchings or explosions, more nearly resemble the pantings of a lion or tiger, than any other sound that has vibrated my ear.

As the train moves off, it rumbles over the first of sixty-three bridges on the line: the iron Water Street Bridge, usually credited to George Stephenson, but probably designed by Jesse Hartley, and built by Manchester industrialist William Fairbairn. Both Stephenson and Fairbairn were Unitarians and their friendship had begun twenty-seven years earlier, in around 1803. By the mid-1820s, Fairbairn was one of the country's leading engineers, much of his reputation stemming from his success as a builder of iron-framed, fireproof buildings.

Construction began during April 1830 and it used revolutionary technology at the time, the Hodgkinson Beam, which had been developed in Manchester by Eaton Hodgkinson. He was a Manchester physicist, who, from *c.* 1820 had been investigating ways to improve

The 1992-built replica *Planet* coupled to the original 'Manchester & Birmingham' first-class coach, 5 January 2016.

WATER STREET RAILWAY BRIDGE, MANCHESTER. BUILT 1829.

LNWR postcard of the Water Street Bridge, looking south, prior to its demolition in 1904. Bears comparison with the scene 112 years later. (Author's Collection)

The junction of Liverpool Road and Water Street. It is worth comparing with the same view by Thomas Bury (1835) on page 35. The station agent's house is visible on the right; in the centre of the view is the new Water Street Bridge of 1904 (replacing that of 1829–1830) and on the left is the sloping ramp that led down from rail level to the abattoir on Water Street. (Author)

cast-iron beams. Hodgkinson's work attracted first Peter Ewart, another Manchester engineer, and then Fairbairn and his business partner James Lillie to develop the Hodgkinson Beam further. It had originally been planned to separate the road from the foot way with a stone wall, but instead twenty-two cast-iron fluted Doric columns – weighing 45 tons – were installed. The bridge was demolished in 1904 as part of a programme to replace cast girder railway bridges.

After having crossed Water Street, the train rolled through the arrival station, opened on 4 December 1837, in order to ease congestion and confusion at Liverpool Road with passengers – and trains – trying to arrive and depart at the same time from the same cramped accommodation. This was a situation that would have been made worse following the introduction of through-trains from Birmingham via the Grand Junction Railway in 1837. The Liverpool & Manchester Board noted that some passengers had been alighting from their carriages from the wrong side and trying to cross the railway line or get out at unscheduled stopping places; they therefore ordered all carriage doors to be fitted with locks and only those doors on the platform side to be unlocked at stopping places. This, however, caused consternation following a fire on a French train where the passengers were trapped and burned to death (1837).

The site of the former dyeworks of Rothwell & Harrison was purchased in 1835 and tenders were invited during the following year for the new arrivals station: it was built at a cost of £7,999 by William and Henry Southern to a design of Haigh & Franklin of Liverpool; with the completion of the boundary wall, gates and improvements to the existing Liverpool Road buildings, the total cost in 1838 was £8,600. The new arrival station, opened 4 December 1837, was between Water Street and the Irwell – exactly where the new 'Ordsall Chord' will run and where, to 5 January 2016, the railway volunteers at the Museum of Science & Industry operated their public passenger trains. The arrival station was of two storeys, 156 feet long and 51 feet deep. At rail level, the 'arrival shed' was on the north side of the line, with an overall roof supported on cast-iron columns at 13-foot intervals along the side next to the railway. Access was via two sloping ramps, including a carriage dock to allow the transportation of private carriages. On the south side, there was a water tower, pumping engine and boilers (the locomotives were filled with hot water). The Manchester firm Galloway & Bowman provided the pumping engine to supply the 15-foot-tall water-tower cistern. The engine incorporated one of the cylinders from Stephenson's *Twin Sisters* locomotive of 1829, used in the construction of the line. Beneath the station were stables for sixty-one horses as well as kitchens and mess rooms for the station staff. New stables were built in 1869, now latterly part of Granada Studios, and were in use as late as 1938.

Rolling out of the arrivals station, the train crosses the Irwell Bridge, designed by Jesse Hartley (erroneously credited to Stephenson) and built by David Bellhouse Jnr. Hartley had been previously employed by the Liverpool Harbour Board from 1824 and built or rebuilt every dock in their extensive system over thirty-six years. The outline design for the bridge was ready by September 1828 but the additional Enabling Act of May 1829 was required to commence work. Like the Sankey viaduct, it is built from brick, faced in red sandstone. The contractors almost immediately got into difficulties, the *Manchester Guardian* reporting that the coffer dam built in mid-stream leaked copiously. However, by April, it reported

Thomas Bury's view of the arrivals station, *c.* 1835. Visible are both the Irwell Bridge and Water Street Bridge. The approach ramps and the water tower – fed with hot water and the chimney from the engine house – are prominent. Probably demolished in the 1840s.
(Author's Collection)

A desolate view across Water Street Bridge, after lifting of the MOSI main-line connection and the 'Pineapple Line'. Here was built the 1837 arrivals station. Just visible on the left are the original retaining wall and the concrete platform for animals destined for the Water Street Abattoir.

A fragment of the 1837 arrivals station between the 1904 and 1866–69 Water Street Bridges. Beneath the arrivals platform were mess rooms, a kitchen, and stables for over sixty horses. (Author)

that the dam was dry. There was a further setback when the boat that was used to carry the masons across the river capsized and twelve men were drowned. Construction was well under way by mid-June 1830 when the *Manchester Mercury* reported that

> Since Thursday, the workmen ... have begun to erect the centres of the arch to be thrown across the Salford side of the river, which is now completed up to the foot of the arch.

The first arch was completed by 20 July and the bridge was completed, reported the *Manchester Guardian,* by the end of August. The contract for the bridge had been let to J. B. Brockbank and Alexander Fyfe – the latter was a Scot who was known to George Stephenson, as he had worked with him building bridges on the Stockton & Darlington Railway.

Animals and Livestock

The first goods train – then termed 'Luggage Train' – ran on 4 December 1830, drawn by *Planet* and consisting of 135 bags of American cotton, 200 barrels of flour, sixty-three sacks of oatmeal and thirty-four sacks of malt, loaded in eighteen wagons with a gross weight of 51 tons, 11 cwt 1qr. During the remainder of the month, the Liverpool & Manchester carried some 1,432 tons of freight, a figure rising to 5,104 tons by March 1831. The railway was clearly becoming established as the prime mover not only of people but of light freight. The canals retained the monopoly on bulky and heavy freight such as cotton.

The Liverpool & Manchester began carrying livestock in 1831, usually pigs coming from Ireland via Liverpool; a pig market was established in Grape Street immediately behind the station in the early 1830s. One of the first consignments of livestock was forty-nine pigs (*Manchester Chronicle* 24 May 1831) but, by June, the local press was complaining about the inconvenience caused by the numerous arrivals of cattle, pigs and other livestock at the station. By September 1833 the railway was carrying around 1,500 pigs per week. As a result of this, the Railway Company arranged with George Jones of Pendleton to establish a livestock market between Oldfield Road and Cross Lane, Salford, on land that was owned and crossed by the railway. This new cattle market was opened in July 1837 and

> the Directors of the Liverpool & Manchester Railway Company have agreed to open a slip at the Cross-Lane bridge, to enable dealers to take their cattle upon the road more readily, and in accommodation which is very desirable.

It was at Cross Lane that one George Francis, 'an Irish pig-driver', was killed: the pig wagon in which Francis was travelling was uncoupled from the engine 'for the purposes of being left at Oldfield Road bridge, where livestock is unloaded' and he jumped off the wagon in the belief that 'his pigs were about to be stolen'. He tripped and fell into the path of the pig wagons and 'four carriage wheels passed over his legs, which were dreadfully mangled'. He was taken to the Manchester Infirmary, where he died. Following the cessation of passenger activities at Liverpool Road, the site of the former arrivals station became that for pigs and cattle destined for the abattoir on Water Street; the abattoir was closed in the 1960s but the ramp down to street level still exists (2016).

General merchandise wagons, carrying a variety of goods as depicted by Isaac Shaw. Instead of lounging on the cargo, brakesmen were required to 'ride on the wagon, and keep a good lookout, under pain of dismissal' and 'forbidden to pass over the loaded wagons, to the unavoidable injury of the sheets'. (Author's Collection)

Cattle and pig wagons by Isaac Shaw. Pigs were carried in slat-sided wagons, the owners cramming in as many animals as possible. The 'pig men' were allowed to travel with their beasts for free. The Company charged 25s per pig or cattle wagon. Pigs were often carried in the sheep wagons, as many as fifty squealing, terrified animals being squeezed into a single wagon. In 1841 the Society for the Prevention of Cruelty to Animals reprimanded the Company for its treatment of animals. (Author's Collection)

Liverpool & Manchester sheep wagon, as depicted by Isaac Shaw. Sheep were first carried in October 1831 in these double-decked wagons with a canvas roof. The Company initially charged per animal but quickly charged per wagon (£1 for a sheep wagon). (Author's Collection)

Some of the most unusual animals to arrive at Liverpool Road were destined for the Manchester Zoological Gardens, opened in 1838 between Broom Lane and Broughton Street, Salford. The *Manchester Courier* reported in April 1838 the arrival of a female Indian Elephant – and her boy attendant – who was

> Marched from the Railway Station, through the streets of Salford, on her way to the Gardens; her young keeper bestrode her, with his pike, directing and guiding the huge animal ... Of course, so novel a spectacle soon attracted a crowd, which increased to great extent ... Her pace was a quick walk, neither trot nor amble ...

Other exotic arrivals were 'two fine leopards, a panther, two Antilles monkeys, a common monkey, two Indian sheep, a boa constrictor, and specimen of the *cobra di capello*, or hooded snake'. All were safely delivered to the Zoological Gardens.

Fyfe's Yard

Situated between Oldfield Road and Ordsall Lane were the engine sheds for the 'Manchester' or 'Eastern Division' of the railway, managed by Alexander Fyfe, who was appointed in March 1832. Fyfe was responsible for day-to-day repairs and maintenance of the locomotives. His counterpart in Liverpool was John Melling at Brickfield station (Melling's shed). In 1837, Melling was appointed locomotive superintendent with overall superintendence for the locomotives and repair shops. In Manchester, he employed 120 men and boys as machinists, fitters, and lighter-uppers. Engine cleaners, however, were paid for by the engineman out of his own pocket. Enginemen and firemen were appointed to a single locomotive and were not permitted to operate any other; despite this, Ralph Thomson, the driver of *Mars*, was suspended by the directors for refusing to drive *Arrow* – albeit at the director's request – in February 1832, but was reinstated a month later. Cleaning and preparing a locomotive could be a dangerous job, as the *Liverpool Mercury* reported:

> On Wednesday night, a young man, employed in cleaning the wheels of the *Vulcan*, steamer, got his arm so entangled in one of them, that, before he was disengaged, it was

Ordsall Lane Junction in LNWR days. Ordsall Lane became a busy junction following the opening of the Hunt's Bank extension in 1844, curving off to the north to Hunt's Bank, latterly Victoria station. Curving off to the south was the Manchester South Junction & Altrincham Railway of 1849. (Author's Collection)

crushed to a mummy above the elbow. The poor fellow was about a quarter of an hour in this perilous situation, and he bore it with extreme fortitude. He was sent to the Infirmary.

The fitters were paid from 4s 6d to 5s a day, while 'the lads beginning each earn[ed] 9d a day'. Their working hours were from 6 a.m. to 8 p.m., 'with an allowance of half an hour for breakfast, one hour for dinner, and half an hour for bagging (tea-time)'. In the workshops were 'lathes and other machinery', driven by a 6 hp steam engine. By the mid-1830s, the workshops were in 24-hour operation in order to get locomotives serviced, prepared and back out on the road for the following day.

Firemen and enginemen had to sign on at either 45 minutes or half an hour before departure time. Most of the firemen were locals but the enginemen were from the north-east, which lead to considerable resentment from the local workforce – but where else was George Stephenson to find a pool of experienced enginemen to run the Liverpool & Manchester? Enginemen were paid 1s 6d per trip, for up to four trips per day and the firemen 8d. It was from Melling's shed that prospective firemen and enginemen were appointed. A lad would be taken on aged fourteen or so and employed as a cleaner, before being trained as a fitter to get a thorough understanding of the mechanics and repair of a steam locomotive. From there he could be promoted to fireman, and thence engineman. In 1834 the directors stated that:

> In appointing firemen it was desirable to look forward to their becoming enginemen, and with this in view it must be an advantage to a man to have been employed in a fitter's shop. They wished, therefore, that when vacancies occurred, that the firemen should be supplied from the repairing sheds.

Engine sheds – or, as they were referred to in the 1830s, 'depots' and 'engine houses' – were dangerous places. On 21 March 1831, John Burn, a goods guard, arrived at work 'in a state of intoxication' at Liverpool Road station. When walking up the line to Ordsall Lane to meet the wagons, he slipped, fell and was run over, both of his legs having to be amputated below the knee. In the evening of the same day, John Lawrence, who operated one of the turntables, had a stroke, fell onto the track and was run over by an oncoming train. The driver of the train had seen his unconscious body on the track and thought it was a plank or a similar obstruction but had been unable to stop in time. In July 1832 George Smith, who worked at the coal wharves at Liverpool Road, was again walking along the line at Ordsall Lane when he too was run over, and the wheels of the train 'cut his head completely in two'.

Strike Action

In its early years, the Liverpool & Manchester had poor labour relations, largely as a result of it having a monopoly on skilled railway workers. Locomotive crews regularly worked 12-hour days and the first group to complain about pay and conditions were the firemen. In 1832 they complained as a group about the discrepancy in their pay (up to 15s per week) compared to the £2 of the enginemen. The directors responded quickly by sacking the firemen and replacing them with 'stout boys' who would work for the 15s a week. In February 1833, the directors reduced the pay of the locomotive crews as well as their bonuses for making extra trips, and for Sunday working. A deputation of enginemen and firemen attended a management committee meeting, but the directors felt they 'could not respond' and, moreover, that the letter the men had written to them 'was an improper one'. In other words, the men should put up and shut up. The final straw came in 1835 when the directors, recognising the disparity in pay between enginemen and firemen, decided to reduce the wages of the former, rather than raise those of the latter. The enginemen as a group petitioned the directors, urging them to abandon their proposed wage cuts and managed to secure an agreement that their wages would not fall below 30s per week. This, however, did not meet their demands and, when on Monday 30 January 1836 the new rates of pay were introduced, the first railway strike in history was called. Several enginemen had given verbal notice that they would quit; Henry Booth, the secretary and treasurer, wrote to each man giving them a 'cooling off' period of a fortnight but the final straw appears to have been the sacking of one of the most senior of their number, John Hewitt. Faced with a prospect of having no men to work their locomotives, the directors speedily

> Filled up the places from the turn-outs from amongst the mechanics [i.e., fitters], whose previous knowledge of the construction of the engines very soon enabled them to overcome every difficulty in their new vocation.

The men who were taken on to break the strike, in recognition of their service despite the 'persuasions and threats' from their colleagues, were awarded premiums of £5 and £3. Four of the striking enginemen – Henry Weatherburn, Peter Callan, Charles Callan and George Massey – went before the magistrates, who considered 'the offence of so grave a character' that they were sentenced to three months' hard labour on the treadmill at Kirkdale Gaol. The directors hoped that the example made of these four would 'tend powerfully to secure discipline and good conduct hereafter'. The directors, however, soon had to change their tune: with the railway boom of the mid-1830s, the Liverpool & Manchester no longer had the monopoly on skilled railway workers and, only a year after the strike, complained to the Great Western Railway about them 'poaching' some of their best men by offering higher pay. As a result, bonuses and other incentives were introduced to improve loyalty – as well as efficiency (paid for the least amount of coke used) and punctuality.

Policemen, Switchmen and Gatemen

One traveller on the railway in October 1830 noted

> There are men placed at the distance of about two-thirds of a mile from each other, whose business it is to look out for danger and prevent accidents. They have a certain signal which denotes 'all's well', and a small flag which they hoist when the engine arrives in sight, if it be necessary for the train to stop. With these precautions it is next to impossible that any accident should happen.

There were around sixty railway policemen appointed when the railway opened, and they were paid 17s 6d per week, increasing to 32s per week in 1831, when they were also issued winter coats and watch boxes. There was one policeman at each of the eighteen 'stopping places', twenty-one level crossings and the two terminal stations. Also part of the railway police were the gatemen (who opened the crossings gates) and the switchmen, who manually operated the switches. They were chosen from among former soldiers and the best policemen and, because of their responsibility, were better paid than their colleagues (19s per week). Members of the railway police were sworn special constables and were issued with two truncheons, handcuffs, rattle and handcuffs. Switchmen were also issued with crowbars (to help move any reluctant switch blades). They were readily identified through the wearing of blue tailcoats and tall stovepipe hats, with 'Railway Police' painted in gilt letters on the front. In a money-saving exercise in 1832, the number of the railway police was slashed by twenty, so that the intermediate 'stopping places' were no longer manned. This reduction, in the opinion of the Manchester coroner, was responsible for a fatal accident on Parr Moss, 1 March 1833; the number of railway police was only increased in 1837 with the opening of the Grand Junction Railway.

Every railway policeman had three hand flags – white (go on); red (danger/stop); green (caution) – that were used during the day. At night they used a triple-aspect lamp like those used by the guards. A blue flag was shown if a train needed to stop to pick up passengers or goods wagons and, if there were platelayers repairing the permanent way, a black flag was shown.

Mid-Victorian depiction of a railway switchman ('Mind your points' by John Gilbert, 1867), who was responsible for setting the switches before the introduction of interlocking switches and signals. (Author's Collection)

The Permanent Way

It is from the Liverpool & Manchester that Britain derives it peculiar 'standard gauge' of 4 feet, 8.5 inches. George Stephenson originally proposed a gauge of 4 feet, 8 inches, while George Rennie proposed 5 feet. The company's fourth Act stipulated a gauge of 4 feet, 8 inches, 'clear, between the rails', rather than from centre to centre. The Liverpool & Manchester was double track from the start, with the north line carrying trains from Liverpool, the south line trains from Manchester. It is unclear where the extra half-inch came from! Originally the two running lines were separated by 4 feet, 8.5 inches as it was envisaged that extra-wide loads could be thus carried down the centre of the line. When the track was re-laid, the loading space between the running lines was widened to 5 feet, 1 inch.

The railway was initially laid with quite lightweight (35 lbs per yard) fish-bellied rails, 15 feet long, secured to cast-iron chairs that were bolted to stone blocks, 2 feet square. The stone blocks were set diagonally so that their edges nearly touched. Timber sleepers were used on embankments and on Chat Moss, where it was thought the weight of the stone sleepers would cause them to sink. The timber sleepers were initially oak but were later swapped for larch and, by 1839, the whole of the line had been re-laid with larch sleepers in lieu of the heavy stone blocks. To prevent them rotting, the directors purchased a licence for 'Kyan's Patent Process for the Prevention of the Dry Rot'. This was a process developed by John Howard Kyan in 1832 to preserve timber by soaking it in a chemical solution of bichloride of mercury for several days. The same process was later adopted by the Board of Ordnance and the Admiralty.

As early as 1832, there were numerous reports of broken rails throughout the line caused by the weight of locomotive such as *Planet* or *Samson* and other increasingly heavy trains. Experiments were carried out in 1833 on different types of rail but, despite 'malleable iron' rails being conclusively proved to be the superior type, rolled iron rails weighing 50 lbs per yard were ordered in November 1833. In 1834 the directors experimented with parallel rail and, over a period of eighteen months, their performance was compared with fish-bellied rails. John Dixon reported in June 1835 in favour of fish-bellied rail, weighing 55 lbs per

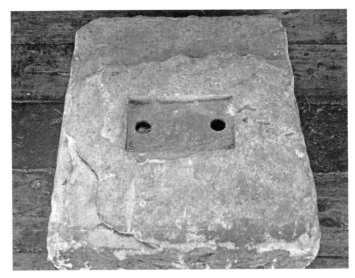

A stone sleeper block; an iron chair was bolted to the block, and the rail then keyed to the chair. The use of stone blocks was an anachronistic move by George Stephenson, who preferred them to wooden sleepers. Wooden sleepers were used on Chat Moss and on embankments where the heavy stone blocks were likely to sink.

yard, carried in an iron chair. Having concluded that the entire line would need to be re-laid, they began to make preparations for the colossal project late in 1835 and new rails began to be laid in the New Year of 1836. Due to the increasing cost of iron, the directors resorted to an Act of Parliament (5 May 1837) for powers to raise the additional funds for laying the line with even heavier 75-lb parallel rail at a cost of £14 5s per ton. The project was completed by 1838. The Whiston and Sutton inclines were re-laid with parallel rails weighing 60 lbs per yard in 1838. In order to help fund this work, the old rails and chairs were sold for scrap.

Manchester to Chat Moss

The Liverpool & Manchester was primarily an inter-city passenger railway; according to Henry Booth in 1841, 'the intermediate stations are of so little importance on our line, we have there few but policemen'. He reported to the Parliamentary Select Committee on Railways that

> We have twenty stopping places ... we do not stop at all places, but we sometimes stop at six or eight ... but if we were to be limited to a timetable, we must be stopping at every one of the twenty stations ... Our man merely has to open and shut the gate; the train stops, takes up the passengers, and goes on.

Between Manchester and Chat Moss were five 'stopping places' in 4 miles: Ordsall Lane, Cross Lane, Weaste Lane, Eccles and Patricroft. Facilities were primitive, usually a wooden

Eccles Station photographed in LMS days, probably a century after it had first opened as an intermittent stopping place on the Liverpool & Manchester. It was here that the wounded William Huskisson was rushed on the opening day, and thence to Eccles Rectory, where he later died. (Author's Collection)

running-in board and gates across the line but nothing more. A wooden hut was erected at Cross Lane in 1832 and at Patricroft, which was later rebuilt in brick in 1838. Improved facilities were built at Patricroft in 1841. The number of 'stopping places' was quite variable through the first decade of the company's existence and it was only gradually that facilities were improved for passengers.

All of the 'stopping places' were next to roads, the gateman who was in control of the level crossing being responsible for hosting a red – later blue – flag up the flag pole if a train was ordered to stop to pick up passengers or goods wagons. The gateman, in addition to opening and closing the gates across the line, was responsible for setting the colour of the gate lamp: white for 'go on' and red for 'set down'. Very often the gatekeeper's cottage next to the line was used as waiting accommodation for passengers; at Rainhill, one of the busier 'stopping places', the gateman was allowed an extra ton of coal to provide some warmth for the passengers. In 1832 a larger waiting room was built there at a cost of £127. A permanent 'cottage' (i.e. waiting room) was built at Broad Green in 1832 and the temporary wooden hut re-erected at Cross Lane, just outside Manchester. Other 'cottages' were built at Flow Moss, Kenyon Junction and Parkside – the latter being the principal watering and re-coaling station on the line. A cottage was built either side of the line at Newton Junction. In order to sell tickets at the 'stopping places', one of the guards was issued with a large, lockable, leather satchel from which he issued tickets and collected the fares. The name of the station and number of passengers that had boarded the train was written on a slip and deposited in a pouch on the satchel. At the terminal stations, the satchel handed in to the booking office, where the fares collected were checked against the number and type of ticket sold.

CHAPTER 3

Bogs and Bridges

Chat Moss

The first major obstacle to be crossed was the vast expanse of Chat Moss. Walker in 1831 described it as '... this heathy ocean, the prospect is somewhat bleak and cheerless'. The first attempts to drain the moss were made in 1793 by William Roscoe and his steward, a Mr Wakefield of Liverpool, under the Enclosure Act. In order to drain the Moss, numerous deep drains had been cut through it and a light wagon way had been laid across its surface. Around 1816 Robert Stannard improved the wagon way across the Moss to carry peat and turf for fuel. A pamphlet published in 1844 ('The Way to Reclaim Mosses') suggests that Roscoe was aided by three factors in reclaiming the moss: 'the simple yet scientific appliance of materials hostile in their nature to that of the moss (Mr Roscoe used marl and sandy gravel)'; secondly, 'a sufficiency of money to pay the expenses of these materials'; and finally, 'a security that he would reap the benefits ... which security can at all times ... enable ... to borrow money from the banks'.

A lone train crossing the bleak Chat Moss, as depicted by T. T. Bury in the 1830s. (Author's Collection)

Work commenced in 1826 when Vignoles had staked out the entire route across the Moss; the land the railway was to cross was purchased from a Mr Borron, 100 yards wide and 4 miles long at £2 per acre; the cost for the 4-mile-long strip being less than £300. Robert Stannard (above) was employed as the major contractor, cutting the drainage ditches. He also had the contract for the cutting between Eccles and the Moss. Other contractors included a Mr Blacklock and a Mr Willy. The *Liverpool Advertiser* (7 July 1826) notes that work had commenced at Chat Moss 'to prepare for that part of the line'. In order to transport workers and materials along the moss, a temporary light railway was laid, as reported by *The Examiner* (30 December 1827):

A Temporary Railway has just been laid over the whole length of the Moss, which serves to bring in materials and to convey the work-people and superintendents with great facility. Every morning and evening the wagons are seen hurrying along at the rate of six miles an hour with ease; a single man will convey by this means eight or ten of his fellow-workmen at the rate of six miles an hour with ease, and one active fellow, more swift of foot than his companions, last week pushed a wagon, containing ten passengers, across the Moss, a distance of four miles and a half, in the short period of thirty minutes.

Drainage ditches were dug parallel to the railway, but problems arose when their soft sides kept collapsing: it was overcome by using empty tar barrels from Liverpool, which were laid end-to-end and sealed with clay to form a continuous wooden culvert to carry off the water. As the ground became dryer and more stabilised, a mat of tree trunks and branches was laid, which were covered with layers of heathers and moss, interspersed with more layers of brushwood hurdles to form the base of the 'floating' road bed. As the moss was drained, and began to dry out, it naturally contracted, as reported by the *Westmoreland Gazette* (17 July 1830):

A house and farm building ... were erected on the edge of the Moss; during the building of which, a curious circumstance occurred, which marked the effect of the drainage in a striking manner. From one of the rooms in the house, the sails of a wind mill on the rising ground on the opposite side of the moss began gradually to show themselves, and in the process of time, by the operation of the drains, the surface subsided, so as to let in view, not only the whole mill, but of a large tract of country which before was hidden by the intervening moss.

Around 200 men worked on the Moss, and progress was initially quite rapid but was disrupted by the harsh winter of 1826–1827. Chat Moss was unstable to a depth of 10 to 35 feet, but at a site called 'black pool hole' the bottom could not be found. Wagonload after wagonload of spoil (from the nearby cutting) was tipped into the morass for more than three months without making an apparent progress. The directors, quite naturally, became alarmed at the delay and increasing cost. Stannard advised them to purchase a plantation of young larch trees at Botany Bay Woods, near Worsley, which were laid 'herringbone fashion' to form a solid mat, upon which tons of rock and gravel were tipped.

A similar tactic was used at either end of the Moss to build the embankments: some 670,000 cubic yards of spoil were tipped into the bog, interlayered with brushwood

LNWR postcard from 1905, depicting seventy-five years of railway progress. Compare the first-class rail travel in 1835 with the 'American Special', which ran from Euston to Liverpool Riverside, beginning in 1895, carrying first-class passengers to Liverpool Docks for their Atlantic crossing. (Author's Collection)

hurdles, creating a solid embankment. Several 'stopping places' were opened on the moss, at Barton Moss, Lamb's Cottage, Bury Lane and Flow Moss, which were all in intermittent use. Barton Moss had opened by 1831 but closed in 1862 when it moved to a different location, slightly further the east. It closed in 1929. Bury Lane (latterly 'Glazebury and Bury Lane') opened by March 1831 and closed in 1958, by which date it sported a typical LNWR timber platform building. Astley station, contiguous to Rindle Road, had opened by 1844 and closed in 1956.

Crossing the Moss took nearly three years at a cost of £27,719 11s 10d, making it the cheapest section of the line and considerably less than the £200,000 that the engineer Francis Giles had estimated before parliament in 1825. The *Manchester Times* (10 January 1829) reported how,

> The railway extends four miles along the Moss... and where two years ago man could not walk, horses are now dragging loads of from six to twelve tons.

Rocket, the winner of the Rainhill Trials, was used on the Manchester to Chat Moss section of the line as a 'ballast engine', pulling permanent-way trains. She was used in a 'most interesting experiment' on Chat Moss in New Year 1830, in order to ascertain the weight the line on the moss could bear:

> Mr Stephenson's loco-motive engine *The Rocket* ... The engine passed westwards to Berry [sic, Bury] Lane, near Leigh, over the whole extent of the Moss, a distance of four miles and a half, with a large train attached of wagons and passengers, in seventeen minutes; and returned, at a speed amounting to twenty-four miles an hour, but diminished at pleasure where the road was incomplete. The Experiment had the effect of completely proving the solidity of the work on a part where it was asserted by many engineers that a foundation could never be obtained. (*Manchester Courier* 2 January 1830)

Rocket 'crossed and re-crossed the Moss' and on the return leg toward Manchester, at Eccles, 'at the rate of twenty-four miles an hour,' she 'was thrown off the road' by one of

A well-known LWNR postcard, purporting to show George Stephenson and *Rocket*. This replica of *Rocket* was built by the LNWR in 1881 at Crewe as part of the Stephenson Centenary celebrations of that year. It was built using the drawings prepared by J. D. Wardale in 1858–1859, who erroneously thought the firebox had a sloping back. The replica was on outside display for many years but its metal components were used in the 1979 Locomotion Enterprises replica for the Rocket 150 event. (Author's Collection)

her iron-carrying wheels breaking. This 'threw off' the 'water-carriage [i.e. tender] and some of the wagons'. None of the 'forty individuals riding in and upon the wagons ... received the slightest hurt'. It appears that *Rocket* had been derailed before, as the broken carrying wheel had 'been previously injured by a carriage purposely thrown off the railway.' *Rocket* was speedily repaired:

> Immediately after the accident a fresh wheel was substituted for that which was broken, and in three quarters of an hour, the engine was again started, and performed its work with accustomed facility.

On the following day *Rocket* repeated the experiment, drawing a load of 35 tons 'with which there was not the least sinking'. The *Liverpool Times* thought that this accident proved how safe the railway was:

> The fact that the carriage being thrown off the railway, and even having one of its wheels broken, did not occasion an overthrow, or any other accident, and that it was so easily stopped when going at so extraordinary a speed, are proofs that travelling rapidly on the railway will be by no means so dangerous as many persons have supposed.

One passenger in October 1830 agreed, describing the railway as far safer than the stage coach:

> Stage-coaches may, as heretofore, be faced with impunity by grown people; they merely run over little children ... But who has not shuddered over the perusal of that appalling, yet concise paragraph which has lately gone round of the newspapers, describing the dreadful overthrow of the Worcester *Aurora*, when nine persons were killed and wounded? And I may ask, who is there of the age of twenty-one and upwards, that has not been overturned or *nearly* overturned, when travelling by the Coach? For my part, I have been *twice* upset, and a thousand times in imminent danger of it; and I will venture to assert on the strength of my own experience, that the degree of danger in travelling on a turnpike road by the mail, or a stage-coach, is ten times as great as on the Manchester & Liverpool Railway at the tail of a steam engine, and certainly not half so comfortable or entertaining.

It is little wonder, then, that most of the twenty-two stagecoaches that ran between Manchester and Liverpool went bust by New Year 1830.

Further 'experiments' were carried out on Chat Moss in April 1830, when *Rocket* hauled a load of 45 tons, 'this by far the greatest weight that has yet been conveyed across the Moss'. The experiment 'proved the sufficiency of that part of the railroad' to support heavy loads at speed, with *Rocket* attaining a speed of 16 miles per hour.

Rocket was involved in an accident while on ballast duties on 28 October 1830, resulting in the death of one Henry Hunter, a local publican who had been riding on her tender. He was a habitual nuisance, in the 'habit of riding backwards and forwards on the engines or wagons, notwithstanding the remonstrances of the engineer'. Having missed the last passenger train, he had caught a lift on the tender of *Rocket* from Salford to Chat Moss. After the ballast had been unloaded at Chat Moss, *Rocket* was propelling her train back towards Salford when one of her tender wheels broke; Hunter was thrown off and was 'killed on the spot' 'by the water cask falling on him'. The engineman was 'violently thrown forward' and received a 'severe wound on the forehead'. Hunter's body was taken to Eccles station, where it presented 'a horrid spectacle'.

Parkside

Parkside was the watering and refuelling point, midway along the line. It was provided with two water cranes, which delivered hot water (Francis Wishaw reported it was 84° F (28° C)) supplied by a boiler installed for that purpose. A 'cottage' as waiting accommodation was erected by 1831. With the opening of Kenyon Junction for the Wigan Branch Railway in 1832 – later part of the North Union, formed in 1834 – and through running from Birmingham (1837) a new station was built in 1839, further east of the original site at the head of a triangular junction. Parkside is best known as where William Huskisson MP was run over by *Rocket*. An impressive memorial tablet was erected to him at Parkside station. Parkside closed to passengers as early as 1878. The 1839 station building was still standing in the 1930s. Huskisson was not the only person to be run down and killed by a train at

Parkside: in August 1832, George Sudlow, a Manchester shopkeeper, despite being told to remain seated in a second-class carriage, 'persisted in standing' and fell out of the carriage. 'It was supposed that he had foolishly tried to quit the carriage while the train was in motion.' One leg was severely fractured, as was his skull. He died in Liverpool Infirmary, leaving a widow and children. For a period between 1847 and 1864, the section from Newton (where the Grand Junction route to Birmingham via Crewe met the Liverpool & Manchester) and Parkside (for Preston via Wigan) was part of the West Coast Main Line, travelling over the Parkside west curve.

'Parkside Station' by T. T. Bury, showing a first-class train taking on water. Parkside became the principal watering point on the line: two water cranes were built, and the engine house used to heat and pump the water is visible on the right. Also shown is the cottage (built 1831–2) to provide waiting accommodation for passengers. (Author's Collection)

The site of Parkside station in 2016; other than the Huskisson Memorial, nothing remains to remind modern railway travellers that there was ever a station here. (Author)

The memorial at Parkside erected at the spot where William Huskisson MP was run over by *Rocket*. (Author)

THE HUSKISSON MEMORIAL WINDOW, IN CHICHESTER CATHEDRAL.

The memorial window to William Huskisson at Chichester Cathedral, given by his wife in 1855. (Author's Collection)

Sankey Viaduct

No fewer than sixty-three bridges were built on the Liverpool & Manchester, ranging from the imposing nine-arch Sankey viaduct to a cattle bridge, carrying the line over a 9-foot farm track. The Sankey viaduct was initially designed by George Stephenson, his first rough sketch for it being included in a letter to Robert dated 23 February 1827. The directors, however, were not very impressed with Stephenson's 'Gothick' confection and they asked Jesse Hartley – their civil engineer – to confer with Stephenson on the matter. The viaduct was completed by Hartley under the direction of William Allcard and Alexander Fyfe (Chapter 2). Work commenced late in 1828 when driving the 200 piles for the foundations of the piers was begun. Each pile had to be driven 20 to 30 feet through the soft, alluvial valley floor in order to stabilise it to take the massive weight of the structure above. By early summer 1829 the piers had been completed, built of brick but faced with local red sandstone: it had originally been Hartley's intention for them to be solid stone but, either due to cost, ease of construction or weight, they were altered to brick. William Huskisson MP visited the railway in August, when he crossed the partially completed viaduct, one arch remaining unfinished. The viaduct was approaching completion by February 1830 when the parapet walls were in position, with the majestic structure towering 60 feet above the valley floor.

Approaching from Newton, trains first crossed the four-arch viaduct at Newton. Essentially a smaller version of the Sankey viaduct built in brick, it carried the line

Sankey Viaduct, as depicted by T. T. Bury in 1831. James Scott Walker waxed lyrical: 'The St Helens Canal passes under one of these noble arches; a small river under another, and the picturesque appearance of vessels under sail, far below ... wending their way ... conveys an impression ... at once pleasing and sublime.' (Author's Collection)

The Sankey Viaduct, depicted from the valley floor showing the Sankey Canal, a.k.a. Sankey Brook Navigation, part of the St Helens canal. It opened in 1757, linking the expanding town of St Helens with the Mersey at Widnes. The canal was built for tall-masted 'Mersey Flats', the traditional sailing vessels of the north-west. The canal closed in 1963. (Author's Collection)

Sankey Viaduct in 2016, striding across the Sankey valley; it is little changed in 185 years. (Author)

Although now somewhat marred by overhead wires, smoke blackened and covered in graffiti, the viaduct is still a grand reminder of the scale of the work to build the Liverpool & Manchester Railway. (Author)

The lovely brick viaduct at Newton-le-Willows, carrying the Liverpool & Manchester over the road, and Old Mill Dam, with four arches 30 feet wide and 27 feet high. It was completed at a cost of £5,340 12s 5d. (Author)

Newton-le-Willows station, opened in 1830 as 'Newton Bridge' and renamed as Newton-le-Willows in 1888. The current Tudor-style buildings date from 1844–45 (built at a cost of £400) and was once a main calling point on the Anglo-Scottish expresses. (Author)

above the Newton and Warrington Turnpike road and the old Mill Dam at a height of 27 feet. The line was carried into the Sankey valley on a 40-foot embankment. 'A Tourist' wrote of the viaduct and embankment in 1831:

> ... the railway is carried at some distance south of the town by a handsome stone bridge of four arches, each 30 feet span, and 27 in height ... Immediately below this bridge stands an old corn mill, and adjacent to it is an antique mansion, displaying in its pointed gables and oak crossings the architecture of Elizabeth's reign. The effect of these objects as viewed from the elevated road is strikingly picturesque.
>
> Still continuing the ascent ... speedily approach the valley of the Sankey, situated about half way between the two extremes of the journey. The railway is carried over this valley along a magnificent viaduct of nine arches, each 50 feet span, and 70 feet above the surface of the ground. This fine structure ... forms not only a chief feature in the beauty of the road, but a very considerable item in the entire cost [£45,200].

After passing through Newton, the line came to the triangular junction at Earlestown – originally named Newton Junction – where the Warrington & Newton railway diverged to the south. The junction opened in 1831 and, from 1837, was where trains from Birmingham via the Grand Junction Railway joined the Liverpool & Manchester.

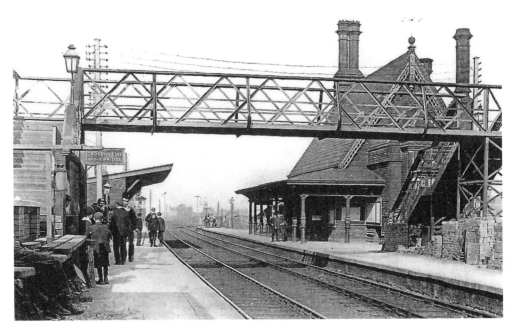

Earlestown station, seen here in Edwardian days. Originally named 'Newton Junction', it was the site of the junction for the Warrington & Newton Railway opened in 1831, which became a key link of the Grand Junction Railway in 1837. It was renamed Earlestown in 1837 after company director Sir Hardman Earle, who developed and expanded the Newton Wagon Works from 1833. After 1853 Earlestown was the focus for wagon repairs on the LNWR; a model town was built for its workers, who numbered 2,000 in 1901. (Author's Collection)

Earlestown station in 2016, pretty much unchanged in a century. The lovely Tudor-style buildings from 1844–45 were restored in 1980. (Author)

Inspection of the Line

The directors visited and inspected the line on Monday 14 June 1830. *Arrow* drew a special train weighing 32 tons gross and consisting of two passenger carriages (5 tons) and seven wagon loads of stone (27 tons):

> The carriages passed through the deep cutting [Olive Mount] at a rapid rate, the bridges and sides of the slopes being lined with spectators who had thronged to see the partial opening of this magnificent work. On arriving at the foot of the inclined plane [Whiston] an assistant locomotive engine was attached to the carriages, and the train ascended to Rainhill at a steady pace. At the end of the ascent, the assistant engine [*Dart*] was detached, and 'The Arrow' proceeded forward at a rate of sixteen or seventeen miles an hour. On arriving at the Sankey Viaduct, the speed was decreased, on account of the present unfinished state of the embankment adjoining the bridge, which is not yet sufficiently consolidated. The engine then moved rapidly past Newton, to the Kenyon Excavation, where a fresh supply of water was taken in, occupying about seventeen minutes; afterwards proceeding at about seventeen miles an hour across Chat Moss where the road is in such excellent order as to call forth the admiration of all the Directors, who pronounced it to be as perfect as any other part of the road; and after taking in another supply of water at Eccles, the Engine proceeded to Manchester, where it arrived at six minutes past eleven. The whole time occupied on the journey being two hours twenty-one minutes, which, after deducting time for taking in water &c., leaves two hours and one minute for the time of performing the journey.

Upon arrival at Ordsall Lane, Manchester, the directors alighted to examine 'the bridges and other works constructing in the neighbourhood of Manchester'. They then adjourned to the house of Gilbert Winter Esq. for a 'cold collation'. A special meeting of the directors was held, which resolved unanimously:

The Directors cannot allow this opportunity to pass, without expressing their strong sense of the skill and unwearied energy displayed by their engineer, Mr George Stephenson, which had so far brought this great national work to a successful termination, and which promises to be so beneficial to the country at large ...

The directors returned to Liverpool in the afternoon, attracting even larger crowds than before:

... the carriages ... were greeted by the many thousands of individuals who had collected from the surrounding neighbourhood ... the procession started with two coaches containing from forty to fifty persons, which darted through the dense mass of individuals who thronged the rail-way, passing Chat Moss at a rate of about twenty-two miles an hour, arriving at Edge Hill, Liverpool, (after deducting seven minutes for stoppages &c.), in *one hour and thirty-four minutes!*

Throughout the summer the directors held excursions along the line, largely as a public relations exercise, to show the speed, comfort and, above all, safety of railway. These public relations exercises were, according to the *Liverpool Mercury* (30 October 1829), extremely popular with the public:

The public ... continue to take advantage of the opportunity afforded them by the directors of visiting and inspecting the Tunnel [Wapping Tunnel] on Fridays. The charges for admission ... and a ride on the locomotive engines, are extremely moderate.

The directors lost no opportunity to promote their railway and its locomotives. They announced via the *Liverpool Mercury* on 6 November 1829

Another Exhibition of Mr Stephenson's Steam Carriage the Rocket.
Will take place at Rainhill,
THIS AFTERNOON, at ONE O'CLOCK ...

These experiments were load trials, both on the Rainhill Level and then on the Whiston Incline to ascertain the pulling-power of locomotives and the maximum load that could be safely drawn. On the level,

At the commencement of the experiment, a load of thirty-three tons was attached [to *Rocket*] ... which it drew along for several miles at the rate of thirteen and a half miles an hour. An additional load was then put on, which raised it to thirty-seven and a half tons, and with this, it proceeded at the rate of thirteen three quarters mile an hour ... The enormous load of forty-two tons was then put on, and with this it proceeded at the average rate of fourteen miles an hour!

Later on the same day load trials were made up and down the Whiston Incline, starting from Huyton:

... it was found that with eleven tons it [*Rocket*] travelled the mile and a half in five minutes and thirty-five seconds, or sixteen miles an hour, and with sixteen tons in seven minutes and ten seconds, or twelve and a half miles an hour. These performances far exceed the warmest anticipations of the friends of locomotive carriages ... (*Manchester Courier* 7 November 1829).

Rocket was on show again in December to allow the 'Directors, accompanied by Mr Stephenson, to come along the whole line of the Railway ... on those parts which are complete.'

One of the most famous travellers on one of the special excursions in summer 1830 was the noted actress Fanny Kemble. She exclaimed:

At its utmost speed, 35 miles an hour, swifter than bird flies ... You cannot conceive what a sensation of cutting the air was; the motion is as smooth as possible ... I could either have read or written; and as it was I stood up, and with my bonnet off, 'drank the air before me' ... When I closed my eyes this sensation of flying was quite delightful, and strange beyond description; yet ... I had a perfect sense of security ...

The dress-rehearsal for the opening day was held in the last week of August 1830:

At four o'clock four carriages left the station in Crown-Street, and proceeded through the small tunnel to the open cutting at Edge-Hill, where the *Phoenix* locomotive engine was attached. The number of persons in this was train about 100. Three other carriages, containing about 75, were then attached to the Rocket, which with the Phoenix moved off towards Spekelands, where they waited until three other carriages, containing about 60, were attached to the *Arrow*. This being accomplished, the signal for starting was given, and the three engines moved off in majestic style, after crossing Wavertree Lane where a vast concourse of persons had assembled to witness the sight. The white flag was hoisted, and the speed was increased to upwards of 24 miles an hour ...

The highest speeds on the run were attained by *Phoenix* – she surmounted the Whiston Incline at 15 miles per hour (*Rocket* 'being of smaller dimensions' managed it at 11 mph and *Arrow* at 12 mph). *Phoenix* achieved a maximum top speed of 30 mph, with an average speed of 21 mph.

CHAPTER 4

Inclines and Trials

After crossing Parr Moss, the line ran through Collins Green, St Helens Junction, and Lea Green (Sutton) and, having mastered the ascent, arrived at Kendrick's Cross (Rainhill). Lea Green was a timetabled 'stopping place' from March 1831 and was renamed Sutton in 1844, reverting back to Lea Green four years later. At St Helens the line was crossed by the St Helens & Runcorn Gap Railway, the latter carried by a handsome bridge depicted by Thomas Bury. A waiting room was provided at St Helens in 1835. After having descended the Whiston Incline, trains ran through Huyton Quarry, Huyton Lane, Roby and finally Broad Green, where a cattle depot was opened in summer 1831. Facilities there included a waiting shelter for passengers and a shed to protect the double-deck sheep wagons. Animals were loaded into the wagons using a loading dock where pens had been constructed, enabling them to be driven up the ramp and into the train.

Thomas Bury's depiction of the graceful bridge carrying the St Helens & Runcorn Gap Railway, engineered by Stephenson's great rival, C. B. Vignoles, carrying the Liverpool & Manchester in the early 1830s. (Author's Collection)

The rather unlovely 1970s station building at Broad Green, in the shadow of the M62. Facilities to handle cattle were developed at Broad Green in the early 1830s. It was here on Christmas Eve, 1873, that Brazilian Vice-Consul Joas Baptiste Cafferena was run over and killed by a freight train as he crossed the line to take the 10.40 p.m. train back to Liverpool after enjoying an evening at the Abbey Hotel. Broad Green is now the oldest railway station in Liverpool that is still in regular use. (Author)

Whiston and Sutton Inclines

In order to raise the line up to its summit, the Rainhill Level, trains approaching from Manchester had to ascend at 1:89 the Sutton Incline and approaching from Liverpool the 1:96 at Whiston. Due to concerns whether early locomotives could haul their trains up the inclines, a 'Bank or Help-up Engine' was always on stand-by at the bottom of each incline. Sidings with water tanks were provided at the top of the inclines. *Samson* and *Goliah* were the regular banking engines; *Milo* and *Atlas* being held in reserve. *Lion* and *Tiger* (Todd, Kitson & Laird, 1838) were first employed as banking engines. This was not a popular posting due to the long hours worked by the crews. Company rules and regulations stated that 'luggage trains' were to be divided at the discretion of the engineman.

On the steeper Whiston Incline it was ruled that half the train was to be shunted into a siding at the foot of the incline and the other half taken up and put into the siding at the top. The engine would then run down the incline to take up the other half of the train, which then had to be marshalled at the top. If wagons were left at the foot of the incline, the guard or some other person was to go back along the track 400 yards with a red flag to warn any oncoming train. If there were 'reasons to expect a Carriage Train' coming up, the remaining wagons had to be shunted off the main line. Regulations clearly stated that in all cases 'luggage trains' were to give way to passenger trains. If assistance was required from

Old meets new: the 1992-built replica of *Planet* side by side with the sole surviving original Liverpool & Manchester Railway locomotive, *Lion* of 1838. They are photographed near Water Street Bridge. (Paul Dore)

the banking engine, that locomotive had to push the train from the rear, 'never to go before a train,' wait until the last wagon had passed and clear the switches and then 'immediately follow' and assist the train up the incline 'but no further'. When descending the inclines, enginemen were ordered to 'go no faster than twenty to twenty-five miles an hour' and on no account were to try to make up lost time by speeding on the inclines.

One railway traveller left a graphic account of a locomotive working hard up one of the inclines:

> These belchings ... During the ascent they become slower and slower, till the automaton actually labours like an animal out of breath, from the tremendous efforts to gain the highest point of the elevation. The progression is not proportionate; and before the said point is gained the train is not moving faster than a horse could pace, with the slow motion of the animated machine, the breathing becomes laborious, the growl more distinct, till, at length, the animal appears exhausted, and groans like the tiger, when nearly overpowered in contest with the buffalo.
>
> The moment the highest point is reached ... the pantings rapidly increase; the engine, with its train, starts off with an augmented velocity, and in a few moments is flying ... like lightning, and with a uniform growl or roar, like a continuous discharge of distant artillery.

Accidents

Despite all the regulations and precautions, both inclines were the scenes of several accidents, some fatal. On 6 March 1837 the *Lightning*, driven by engineman Murphy, was on duty as banking engine, assisting a train up the Whiston Incline. It had reached the top of the bank and had gone on to the top of the Sutton Incline, ready to reverse onto the south line. However, before he had completed this manoeuvre, Murphy heard *Milo* and *Orion* coming up on the Whiston Incline; Murphy ran *Lightning* forward, hoping to run ahead, but was struck behind by *Milo*, which ran into *Lightning*'s tender, derailing it. Murphy jumped off his engine without shutting off steam, and the engine, now detached from its tender, ran down the Sutton Incline and continued to run down the line towards Manchester.

Luckily, a railway policeman at Eccles managed to jump onto her footplate and get her safely into Manchester. All three locomotive crews were severely reprimanded by the board of directors.

Owing to a mistaken signal at the foot of Whiston Incline on 23 September 1837, both Up and Down lines were blocked. The fireman of *Orion* signalled to the policeman to instruct the bank engine (*Hercules*) to follow and assist the train up the incline. The driver of the *Hercules*, however, mistook the signal for one to go on ahead of *Orion* and, as *Hercules* drew out of the siding, she collided with *Orion* as she came past, hitting her tender. Both locomotives were derailed and blocked the line in both directions. Passenger trains on both lines were stopped either side of the obstruction and passengers transferred to other trains running in opposite directions. The obstruction was only cleared by 8 p.m. that evening.

Patentee – the unlucky engine

Robert Stephenson & Co. developed their patented locomotive in the mid-1830s. The titular member of the class, *Patentee*, was delivered in 1834, and was the next major step in locomotive development: an enlarged *Planet* type with an extra pair of carrying wheels behind the firebox and improved valve gear, using gabs and four fixed eccentrics rather than a pair of slip eccentrics and dog clutch of *Planet*. *Patentee* was also the first locomotive to have steam brakes (patented by Stephenson on 7 October 1833).

She was, however, an unlucky engine: her fireman was killed at Liverpool Road in January 1837 when trying to uncouple the water hoses between the locomotive and tender. Early on a late January morning in 1838, William Wood, the driver of *Patentee*, ran into the rear of *Phoenix*, which had been left standing on the incline 'owing to a vague signal from a man left on watch while the policeman went to breakfast'. The board imposed a fine of 5*s* to be apportioned between the policeman and the watchman. *Patentee* was involved in a fatal accident at the end of the year, when she exploded on Monday 12 November 1838.

Robert Stephenson's patent locomotive of 1834; the carrying-wheels behind the firebox made the locomotive more stable at high speed (around 30 mph) than the *Planet* type. (Author's Collection)

Patentee was pilot engine coupled to *Fury* (the train engine) at the head of a heavy train of forty-three loaded goods wagons, assisted (banked) from the rear by the newly arrived *Lion*, driven by Joseph Greenall. While toiling up the incline, *Patentee* blew up with an explosion 'which is stated to have resembled the firing of a cannon, was heard at Prescot and other places, more than a mile distant'. According to the *Manchester Courier* (17 November 1838), 'the Engine was shattered to pieces, and the tubes were totally destroyed'. The engineman, Charles Warburton, was found

> ... not less than forty yards distant ... Lying in a field on the right side of the road, his right leg was broken, and his head terribly mangled ... The Fireman, whose name is Samuel Jones, a lad of not more than eighteen years of age ... was found in the opposite direction. His left leg was literally severed from his body, and lay two yards distant from it.

A railway night-watchman named William Thomas had heard the train approaching, 'regularly beating up the hill' when the boiler exploded. He saw *Patentee* 'flying past him' and on approaching her saw

> ... the engine detached from its tender. There was no engineer or fireman with it. The back of the engine (the fire part) was blown away, and one of the tubes hanging out.

One witness suggested that the crew of *Patentee* had tampered with the Salter safety valve by hanging extra weights on it to increase the boiler pressure – strictly against company regulations. John Melling, the locomotive superintendent was called as witness and could not account for the explosion: he stated that 'if there had been a scarcity of water, the leaden "plug" would have melted, and the fire have been put out'. The boiler plates were both found to have been sound and Melling dismissed the idea that the crew had put extra weights on the safety valve as 'Warburton was an old and experienced engineer' and, furthermore, because *Patentee* had two safety valves – as did all locomotives on the Liverpool & Manchester. One used as a failsafe 'placed out of control of the engineers' made it more unlikely that *Patentee*'s boiler burst due to one safety valve being tampered with.

At the inquest it was found that Warburton had wanted to divide the train to run it up the bank, but had been persuaded not to by Greenall. A verdict of accidental death was recorded and a Deodand – a medieval custom of placing a fine on any property that had taken human life – of 20s was placed on *Patentee*. Despite the inquest blaming tampering with the safety valve, it is likely that the cause of the explosion was due to a fault inherent in the design of both the Planet and Patentee Classes: the drag-pin was riveted directly to the back of the firebox, rather than to the frames so, when under extreme load as *Patentee* was, the firebox could be literally ripped apart. The boiler was by all accounts intact and undamaged but the firebox back plate and wrapper were destroyed, suggesting a catastrophic failure of the firebox. This argument is made more compelling as John Melling reported to the directors that it was the 'outer casing' that had burst. Following the explosion, the directors recommended that 'the staying of the Fire Box above the Fire Door and Boiler End next the Chimney were strong', again suggesting the cause of the explosion lay not with the boiler but the firebox.

Rainhill

Perhaps the most famous name in railway history – the station opened in September 1830, when it was originally several hundred metres further east, at Kendrick's Cross. The railway is spanned by the famous skew bridge, designed by Jesse Hartley, to allow the Liverpool-Warrington-Manchester Turnpike to cross the line. It was described as 'of very curious and beautiful construction' and 'one of the most remarkable skew bridges' in the country – the bridge is built at the acute angle of 34° to the line and was the most acute of the fifteen skew bridges on the route. Work started on the bridge in late 1828, which was completed in 1829: the misleading inscription reads

Isaac Shaw's depiction of the skew bridge at Rainhill in 1831 with a *Planet*-type locomotive hauling a 'luggage train.' (Author's Collection)

The unchanging face of Rainhill's skew bridge, seen here in 1904. (Author's Collection)

Rainhill bridge in 2016. The parapet was controversially raised in 2012 to allow electrification of the route. (Author)

Rainhill is perhaps best known as the scene of the famous locomotive trials of October 1829; trials that decided the future of the railways, and were not without some controversy. The directors had not, by mid-1828, decided upon means of propulsion for the railway; Henry Booth noted,

> Multifarious schemes were proposed to the Directors ... from all classes of persons ... England, America, and Continental Europe were alike tributary ... The Friction of the carriages was to be reduced so low that a silk thread would draw them ... Hydrogen gas and high-pressure steam ...

The whole matter was discussed by the directors in September 1828 when it was decided that one or two of the directors, accompanied by Henry Booth, would visit the Stockton & Darlington Railway to study its operations. They then visited Newcastle to view the colliery lines there: this gave George Stephenson the opportunity he had been waiting

Rainhill station in the 1970s, photographed from the famous Skew Bridge. (Author's Collection)

The immaculate 1840s station buildings at Rainhill in 2016. (Author)

for to demonstrate the superiority of the steam locomotive. James Walker (of Limehouse, London) and John Urpeth Rastrick (of Stourbridge) were ordered to undertake a study of the benefits between fixed engines and locomotive engines: on 13 and 14 January they inspected the Liverpool & Manchester, on 15 January the Bolton & Leigh, and in Leeds at the Middleton Railway they inspected a Blenkinsop locomotive a day later. From Leeds they visited the Stockton & Darlington (17–20 January) and thence to the collieries around Newcastle (Hetton, Brunton & Shields, Killingworth). They reported to the directors in March 1829, concluding cautiously in favour of stationary engines. Following this disappointing news, George and Robert Stephenson and Joseph Locke spent the remainder of the month evaluating locomotives versus stationary engines. Stephenson senior stated: 'Locomotives shall not be cowardly given up. *I will fight for them until the last. They are worthy of a conflict.*' Stephenson believed that stationary engines could in no way 'be adapted to a public line of railway ... they can never do for coaching'. They reported, in April 1829, in favour of locomotives. In the light of these conflicts, the directors decided on 20 April 1829 to offer a premium of £500 for

> A Locomotive Engine which shall be a decided improvement on those now in use, as respects the consumption of smoke, increased speed, adequate power, & moderate weight ...

Rocket Men

The directors appointed a preparation committee consisting of James Cropper, Joseph Sanders, William Rotherham, Robert Benson and John Moss to draw up the 'Stipulations and Conditions' for the locomotive trials dated 25 April 1829. It is likely that George Stephenson, as the company's chief engineer, was consulted in the drafting of them.

The stipulations for the competition were very stringent: the locomotive had to 'consume its own smoke'; had to be carried on springs; have two safety valves; a boiler pressure of no more than 50 psi; have a mercurial pressure gauge; be carried on six wheels and weigh no more than 6 tons; and be capable of pulling a load of 20 tons gross at 10 miles per hour. The trials were to be held on the Rainhill Level, 1.75 miles long, in October 1829.

Rocket visited the Museum of Science & Industry, Manchester, in 2010 to celebrate the 180th anniversary of the Liverpool & Manchester. The 1979-built replica and its train look very much at home in front of the 1830 Warehouse at Liverpool Road station. While *Rocket* certainly ran in primrose yellow at Rainhill, it was probably painted olive green like the rest of the Liverpool & Manchester locomotives in revenue-earning service; indeed, the oldest surviving paint on the original *Rocket* is dark green. (Lauren Jaye Gradwell, 2016)

Three judges were appointed: Nicholas Wood (chief engineer, Killingworth Colliery), John Urpeth Rastrick and John Kennedy of Manchester (cotton spinner, inventor, and one of the founders of the Railway Company).

Four steam locomotives were entered: *Perseverence* by Timothy Burstall of Edinburgh; *Novelty* by Captain John Ericsson and John Braithwaite of London; *Sans Pareil* by Timothy Hackworth of Shildon; and lastly *Rocket* entered by Henry Booth and the Stephensons. Of these four, *Rocket* was the only locomotive to have been built in a specialist factory and was the only one to have been run and tested before the trials.

Rocket was effectively a lighter version of *Lancashire Witch* (1828) – in which Booth had had a hand designing – and built by a consortium of George and Robert Stephenson and Henry Booth. There was a whisper of controversy around them: Booth and George Stephenson were high-ranking officials of the company and stood to benefit financially from *Rocket* winning the trials. Booth and Stephenson shared the Unitarian faith, as did the two founders Joseph Sanders and John Kennedy. The *Liverpool Chronicle* levelled charges of corruption against Booth and the Stephensons, suggesting the Rainhill Trials

The 1929 Science Museum-built replica of Braithwaite & Ercisson's *Novelty*, incorporating one cylinder and four wheels, which had been presented to John Melling and preserved by him in 1833. Her second cylinder is on long-term display at Rainhill Library. A working replica was built in 1979 and showed that *Novelty*, like other forced-draught locomotives, used more power to drive the bellows than her wheels, leaving *Novelty* chronically under-powered. (Matthew Jackson)

The original *Sans Pareil* at the NRM outpost in Shildon. The original locomotive was purchased by the Liverpool & Manchester from Hackworth for £500 but then sold in 1832 to the Bolton & Leigh Railway, where it successfully ran until 1844. It was then used as a colliery pumping engine until 1863. It was restored in 1864 and presented to the Patent Office Museum (now the Science Museum). She was rebuilt in 1837 with new cylinders (8 inches in lieu of 7) and smaller wheels (4 foot replacing 4 foot, 6 inches). (Lauren Jaye Gradwell, 2016)

Replica *Rocket*, drawing a mixed passenger train of the 1830s at Liverpool Road. *Rocket,* however, appears rarely to have been used for passenger trains, being obsolete by the time the railway opened in September 1830. (Lauren Jaye Gradwell, 2016)

were a publicity stunt. Further allegations were levelled at the directors of the Liverpool & Manchester that they were showing favouritism toward their co-religionists.

Kennedy was part of Manchester's business and social elite, which was centred on the radical Mosley Street Unitarian Chapel, whose members included industrialist Edmund Potter (Beatrix Potter was a descendent), Robert Hyde Greg (owner of Quarry Bank Mill, a proprietor of the Company and related to William Rathbone), the engineer Peter Ewart (Chapter 2: he was employed by Greg as engineer from the 1790s), and Kennedy's business partner, James McConnel. William Fairbairn and Eaton Hodgkinson (Chapter 2) were also Manchester Unitarians. Most were members of Manchester's leading institution, the 'Manchester Literary and Philosophical Society', whose members were invariably Unitarians, and included David Bellhouse (Chapter 1) and even James Watt Jnr. Joseph Sanders was a wealthy corn merchant and member of the Paradise Street Unitarian Chapel in Liverpool, together with the Booth family. Other Unitarian directors included James Cropper, William Rathbone and William Wallace Currie. George Stephenson had been educated by the Unitarian Minister, Rev. William Turner of Newcastle, and attended the Dissenter's Chapel in Wylam, which had been founded by James Walker, a Unitarian iron founder of Newcastle. Stephenson had been invited to work for Messrs Losh, Wilson & Bell of the Walker Iron Works as a young man back in 1815. Charles Tayleur, who founded the Vulcan Foundry in partnership with Robert Stephenson, was also Unitarian. Even though *Rocket* was by far the best locomotive at the trials, how much of her victory was a foregone conclusion? Hackworth certainly thought it was, writing that 'the Engine which had a Booth as the inventor ... was, without either judge or jury, to be the winner'.

Part of the tensions between Stephenson and Timothy Hackworth were probably also religious: Hackworth was a devout Wesleyan Methodist, and a lay preacher too, so to him Stephenson would have been a heretic. Hackworth also refused to work on Sundays, while Stephenson had no such qualms. Later supporters of Hackworth blamed the failure of *Sans Pareil* on a burst cylinder, which had been cast by the Stephensons. In fact it was not a cylinder that burst but rather the water-feed pump that failed and the inevitable result was that one of the fusible plugs burned out. However, casting cylinders for the replica *Rocket* and *Sans Pareil*, which involved using floating wooden cores for the valve chest, did prove problematic: eight were cast for *Rocket* in 1979 before a perfect

The 1979-built replica of *Sans Pareil*, in company with *Lion* (No. 57) of 1838 at the 'Rocket 150' event in May 1980. (Author's collection)

pair were found. Back in 1829, six good castings were presented to Hackworth and he was left to take his pick. Ultimately *Rocket* was the superior locomotive: *Rocket* had a heating surface of 117.8 square feet and was able to generate 18.25 cubic feet of steam an hour, while *Sans Pareil* had a heating surface of 74.6 square feet. This was thanks to her revolutionary boiler.

Booth's Boiler

It was Henry Booth who suggested to Robert Stephenson the concept of a multi-tubular boiler: while Booth may have come up with the theory and design, it was down to Robert Stephenson to build it. Booth had designed the twin-flue boiler of *Lancashire Witch* to enable her to burn coke effectively. The 'new plan of boiler' used in the *Rocket* had twenty-five copper tubes of 3-inch outside diameter, probably made by John Abbott of Newcastle. The multi-tubular locomotive boiler had first been conceived eighteen months before in France, by Marc Séguin. Robert Stephenson experienced quite a lot of problem in getting the boiler watertight and then in preventing the ends from deflecting under pressure, having to double the number of boiler stays. The tubes, which connected to the firebox at the rear of the boiler and at the base of the chimney (*Rocket* had no smokebox at this stage), greatly increased the heating surface of the fire by carrying all the hot gasses and smoke from the firebox through the boiler barrel. The blast of the exhaust in the chimney, above the level of the tubes, created a slight vacuum, drawing more hot gases through the tubes, in turn causing the fire to burn brighter as more primary air was drawn through the base of the fire. This world-changing invention gave *Rocket* a far greater steam-raising capacity than any of her rivals. Work had started on *Rocket* by June 1829 and she was completed on 2 September 1829. She was then transported to Killingworth Colliery for testing (3 to 5 September); following this she was returned to Newcastle where Robert carried out a series of tests with differently sized blast pipes to test the effect of their vacuum before modifications were made to the blast pipe on *Rocket*. It was George Stephenson who chose her final colour – yellow – when she was in Liverpool. Her tender was made in Liverpool by the Worsdells (Chapter 2).

The footplate of the replica *Rocket*, showing the very simple controls: valve levers on the left, which had to be manually locked in place; foot pedal for the driving dogs; regulator and water pump. The site glasse and pressure gauge are modern additions. (Lauren Jaye Gradwell, 2016)

She was dismantled, and left Newcastle on 12 September, arriving in Liverpool a fortnight later at Millfield Yard, near Crown Street. Ralph Hutchinson, one of the Stephenson company's fitters, spent the next twenty-two days re-erecting and getting her ready. The Rainhill Trials began on the morning of 8 October 1829, each locomotive entered having to make ten timed round-trips along the Rainhill Level, representing a complete journey from Liverpool to Manchester. When *Rocket* was not employed on the trials, she was used to entertain the crowds and give demonstration runs, and on one occasion (14 October) 'moved at the astonishing rate of 35 miles an hour'. She also managed to ascend the Whiston Incline at between 15–18 mph, pulling a load of thirty passengers, conclusively proving that stationary winding engines were not necessary to work the inclined planes.

Rocket, as history records, was the victor, and the Liverpool & Manchester ordered four *Rocket*-type locomotives from R. Stephenson & Co. on 26 October 1829 (*Arrow, Comet, Dart, Wildfire*), first running in January 1830. They incorporated many lessons learned from *Rocket*:

- Larger driving wheels (5-foot diameter, in comparison to the 4 feet, 8.5 inches of *Rocket*)
- Cylinders inclined at 8 degrees (compared to 38 of *Rocket*)
- Valve chests on top of the cylinders (*Rocket*'s were underneath to prevent priming)
- A steam dome (to prevent priming)
- Internal steam pipe (for greater thermal efficiency)
- Greater number (ninety) of smaller boiler tubes (to increase the heating surface)

Wildfire a.k.a. *Meteor* made its first appearance on Monday 18 January 1830 when it achieved a maximum speed of 30 mph. The contemporary press reported:

The Cylinders are larger, and placed almost horizontally, and the diameter of the wheels is four inches greater ... These alterations are expected to give the new engine greater speed,

North Star – one of six modified *Rocket* designs delivered in 1830: *Arrow* (No. 2), *Wildfire* a.k.a. *Meteor* (No. 3), *Dart* (No. 4) and *Comet* (No. 5) were delivered in New Year 1830, while *North Star* (No. 8) and *Majestic* (No. 10) were delivered during the summer. All six ran on the opening day. (Author's Collection)

and to make its motion more regular and steady. There had also been an improvement made in means of stopping it, by which it may be brought to a standstill almost instantly ...

On her first run, *Wildfire* made a spectacular debut:

> ... it exhibited a grand and imposing sight ... and, as the engine was approaching its maximum velocity, it continued to vomit out from the top of the chimney sparks, and masses of blazing coke, which gave the machine the appearance of a moving volcano, scattering fire-balls and red-hot cinders as it darted along the road, illuminating the air and throwing a transient glare on the countenances of the astonished bystanders ... aptly enough illustrated the name of 'Wildfire' which is given to it.

These four were rapidly superseded in June 1830 by *Phoenix* and *Northumbrian*, which sported an integral firebox and an ash box at the front end – but not yet a smoke-box proper.

The obsolescence of *Rocket* is shown by the fact it had a working life on the Liverpool & Manchester of about four years: she was involved in four accidents, one of them fatal. It was after an accident in January 1831 that she was heavily rebuilt with lowered cylinders and a steam dome. She was hired out to the Wigan Branch Railway (1832) but was involved in

An LNWR postcard of *Northumbrian* (No. 7). Sketched by James Nasmyth (of Steam Hammer fame) on 12 September 1830. When this sketch was first published in 1884, it was thought to show *Rocket* rather than *Northumbrian*, and many at the time believed there had been two *Rockets*, due to the differences between the two locomotives. (Author's Collection)

a serious collision (November) and was under repair until New Year 1833. *Rocket* was used as a test-bed for Lord Dundonald's rotary engines from 1833 to 1834 and finally laid up. *Rocket* was sold in 1836 for use on the Naworth colliery, near Carlisle, until around 1840. *Rocket* remained at Naworth until 1851 when Robert Stephenson & Co. wanted to display her at the Great Exhibition. This never happened and *Rocket* remained at the Stephenson works until 1862, when she was presented to the Patent Office Museum.

Planet Suite

It was Robert Stephenson's *Planet* that first brought together all the key features of the mature steam locomotive: a multi-tubular boiler with a steam dome and internal steam pipe; firebox within the boiler shell and a proper smokebox with blast pipe at the front end. Cylinders were mounted low down, nearly horizontally under the smokebox (to keep them warm to prevent priming), driving a cranked axle. In order to support this axle, Stephenson provided an outer 'sandwich frame', which meant that the main bearings were outside the wheels. There were four inner plate frames between the smoke box and firebox, which each carried a bearing so that the axle was fully supported: the wheels and each of the crank throws were therefore supported between an inner and outer bearing in an attempt to relieve the crank axle of many of its stresses. Despite this, crank axle failure was a common feature on Planet types, of which forty were built worldwide. Following a spate of broken crank axles in 1831, the directors ordered new, thicker, crank axles to be fitted. The replica's crank axle failed following a derailment, which confirmed historical data that the crank axle was indeed poorly designed. The titular member of the class was in fact ready for opening day (15 September 1830) but was trapped on board ship in Liverpool Harbour. *Planet* was finally on the line and being tested in early October: the *Manchester Mercury* notes (12 October 1830),

> During the latter part of the week ... the Planet, a new engine, made by Mr Stephenson, had, by way of trial, travelled the length of the railway ... which has only been put upon the road this week, brought a train of carriages in an hour and 35 minutes ...

On 19 November 1830 the *Liverpool Mercury* reported that

> The Planet, a new Engine, of Mr Stevenson's [sic] construction was tried on Tuesday Last, and was found to surpass the most sanguine expectations of the railway directors, as it reached Manchester from Liverpool in the short space of sixty minutes, which included two minutes, the time employed in taking in water on the road, as usual.

The 1992 replica of *Planet* (No. 9); the original was delivered 4 October 1830. *Planet* was twice the weight, power and speed of *Rocket*, and her later sisters were delivered less than a year earlier.

A view underneath *Planet*, showing the outside 'sandwich frames' and the four intermediate iron plate frames (which also support the slide bars), supporting the crank throws of the driving axle and the eccentric cluster.

Planet had been driven light engine and the 'occasion of this rapid passage was the necessity of the Engine being in Manchester by nine o'clock'. The replica, while undergoing trials at the Great Central Railway, Loughborough, managed to achieve around 40 mph. On 4 December 1830 *Planet* hauled the first load of American cotton into Manchester (total train load was 80 tons gross) in 2 hours, 50 minutes, at speeds of 12–16 mph. On subsequent occasions she

> Has repeatedly, *without any assistance*, taken from fifty to sixty tons of goods up the Huton inclined plane (an elevation of one in 96), at an average speed of about ten miles per hour; a performance which was previously supposed to be quite beyond the powers of a locomotive engine ...

The Planet Class (which eventually totalled forty) was the first mass-produced class of railway locomotive. To quote Colonel Steve Davies, '*Planet* compared to *Rocket* was the technological equivalent of the Space Shuttle to Apollo 13'. Due to the unreliability of cast-iron wheels, the first *Planets* had wooden wheels, hooped and flanged with iron. Later locomotives were fitted with wheels using hollow, tapered, wrought-iron spokes, alternately

The footplate and controls of *Planet*. From left to right: steam chest pressure gauge; valve levers; gauge glasses; whistle; regulator; blower (above) injector steam supply (below); Salter safety valve; boiler pressure gauge. The rocking shaft for the valve gear runs horizontally across the firebox back head. Just visible on the left is the reversing pedal, which shifts the driving dogs from left to right to engage forward or reverse gear.

off-set around the centre cast nave. A working replica of *Planet* was built by the Friends of the Museum of Science and Industry, Manchester, between 1986 and 1992, managed by Dr Michael Bailey. It was based on design features from several different members of the class, but using modern materials (the boiler is all-welded with cosmetic rivets) and safety features. The boiler pressure was doubled to 100 psi so that injectors could be used (*Planet* has one injector and one water pump) and the cylinder diameter correspondingly reduced from 11 inches to 7 inches to compensate for the higher boiler pressure. Cast-steel wheels were used. Despite the original locomotive burning coke, it was found that the replica would only steam with coal. A similar problem was discovered with the replica *Rocket* during the re-enactment of the Rainhill Trials at the Llangollen Railway in 2002.

The *Planet* type was quickly modified to create the 0-4-0 Samson Class with 4-foot, 6-inch coupled wheels and an increased cylinder diameter (14 inches) that were inclined so that the connecting rods passed under the leading axle. *Samson* 'made its appearance' by

The author on *Planet* preparing a fireman's breakfast in the traditional manner: bacon and sausages cooked on the shovel. And it tasted delicious!
(Lawrence Cody)

Replicas of *Rocket* and *Planet* running parallel at MOSI: less than twelve months separated the two locomotives, but the advance in design is readily apparent.
(Duncan Hough)

February 1831. The *Manchester Guardian* reported that the 'exploits' of *Samson* completely threw 'into the shade' those of *Planet*; *Samson* 'started from Liverpool with 30 wagons' of 151 tons gross at 8.10 a.m., arriving at Parkside at 9.27 a.m. and Manchester at 10.44 a.m., a total journey time of 2 hours, 21 minutes (which included a stoppage of 8 minutes to take on water). Just as the Planet Class was rapidly developed into the Patentee Class, so too was the Samson class provided with an extra pair of carrying wheels, creating an 0-4-2 or 'Large Samson' class, of which *Lion* (although not in original condition) is a lone survivor of four locomotives to the same design supplied by Todd, Kitson & Laird.

The Samson Class was delivered from February 1831; seven members of the class – *Samson* (No. 13), *Goliah* (No. 15), *Atlas* (No. 23), *Milo* (No. 25), *Titan* (No. 34), *Orion* (No. 35) and *Hercules* (No. 39) – were supplied for the Liverpool & Manchester. (Author's Collection)

CHAPTER 5

Destination Liverpool

Olive Mount Cutting

Having crossed the Roby Embankment, the line cut through the mass of Olive Mount, via a cutting 70 feet deep and only 20 wide, the spoil from its construction being used to make the embankment. Jesse Hartley recommended in May 1827 that some of the 500,000 cubic yards of excavated rock be used for the reconstruction of the Liverpool Docks. Much of the material was also used to make the stone sleeper blocks. It was widened in 1830–31 as the 'stone at each side was valuable'. The line from Liverpool to Huyton was quadrupled in 1871 with the opening of a junction to Wigan at Huyton. This doubled the width of the cutting, and robbed it of much of the dramatic impact it had on Fanny Kemble in 1830:

Thomas Bury's dramatic view of the Olive Mount Cutting in 1831. (Author's Collection)

OLIVE MOUNT CUTTING, NEAR LIVERPOOL.

Olive Mount cutting in 1904 during LNWR days, following the quadrupling of the line; which lost some, but not all, of its dramatic impact. (Author's Collection)

You can't imagine how strange it seemed to be journeying on thus, without any visible cause of progress other than the magical machine, with its flying white breath and rhythmical, unvarying pace, between these rocky walls, which are already clothed in mosses and ferns and grasses; and when I reflect that these great masses of stone had been cut asunder to allow our passage thus far below the surface of the earth, I felt as it no fairy tale was ever half so wonderful as what I saw. Bridges were thrown from side to side across the top of these cliffs, and the people looking down upon us from them seemed like pigmies standing in the sky.

James Scott Walker had been equally impressed:

... a deep and fearful cutting, by which as the wizard, by words, 'Cleft Eldon hills in three,' the Engineer has, by skill, cleft Olive Mount in twain. This cutting, the largest *in stone*, on the whole line, is little short of two miles in length, and is one of the most remarkable portions of the whole undertaking. It is at once unique and picturesque, having the appearance, at its greatest depth, of an immense fosse or ditch, dug out in the perfect rock, of which the hill is composed ... Walled in as it were with solid rock rising almost perpendicularly on each side ... and so diminutive a creeping creature does a man appear at the bottom of the chasm, that the spectator marvels that it is the work of human industry ...

It was in Olive Mount cutting that *Rocket* came to grief in January 1831: one of her driving wheels broke while hauling the 2 p.m. second-class passenger train from Liverpool.

According to the *Morning Advertiser*, the locomotive had been 'incautiously put on the rails ... after the Engineer had reported ... that one of the axles was much bent'. This lead to one of the wheels breaking, causing to the locomotive to derail,

> ... dragging after it the first two carriages, and the rest of the train in consequence being brought to a stand. The effect of this concussion was, that the tender was almost broken to pieces, and the engine itself received considerable damage. Fortunately only two persons (the assistant engineer and a female) sustained any injury, and that not of a serious kind. (*Liverpool Albion* 5 February 1831)

The *Worcester Journal* opined that 'the famous Rocket, by some means or other, got off the rails ... the tender was dashed to pieces against the rocks; the engine considerably injured'. *Rocket* was taken to the Edge Hill workshops for extensive repairs.

Grand Area Edge Hill

Travelling west, through the marl cutting and under the Wavertree bridge, passengers were presented with the magnificent 'Moorish Arch' at the entrance to the 'Grand Area' at Edge Hill. The arch was designed by John Foster and housed the engine houses for the two

Designed by John Foster of Liverpool, the Moorish Arch provided a striking architectural grand entrance to Liverpool but also houses in its base the two winding engines for the Wapping and Crown Street tunnels. It was probably demolished in the 1860s with the widening of the cutting. (Author's Collection)

winding engines for the rope-worked section of the line through the two tunnels to Crown Street and Wapping. This situation had come about because the Town Fathers of Liverpool had forbade the use of steam locomotives within the town; locomotives were detached or coupled on at Edge Hill, causing considerable delay but remaining a feature of railway operations in Liverpool until the 1870s. James Scott Walker waxed lyrical in 1830:

> Arrived at the area behind Edge-Hill, his machine, and many others, are yoked to a charger snorting steam and fire, which, had it been called into existence at the siege of Troy, in place of the colossal wooden toy of Achilles, would have reduced the obstinacy of that devoted city to ten minutes' duration, in place of ten years! In a few moments, the passengers all being seated, the engineer opens the valves, the hissing of steam is suppressed, the engine moves, and is heard as if to pant, not from exhaustion, but from impatience of restraint, the blazing cinders fall behind it, and the train of carriages are dragged along with a sudden and agreeable velocity, becoming as it were, the tail of a comet.

Originally intended to have been built from stone, the Moorish Arch was eventually built from stuccoed brick. The engine houses were 35 feet long and 18 feet wide. They stood approximately 29 feet apart, linked by the decorative arch. Both winding engines were prepared by Robert Stephenson & Co. of Newcastle for £1,600; the first engine was ordered in April 1829 and was to be erected by the first week of November, but the ship carrying it was wrecked off the coast near Aberdeen. The engine was salvaged, however, and was ready by mid-November. Despite this, the directors then claimed £500 against Stephenson & Co. for not delivering the engine on time. It soon became apparent that a second engine was needed and an order was once again placed with Stephenson & Co. for £1,800 in December 1830, who were to supply it within four months. The engine on the north side worked the Crown Street tunnel, while the engine on the south side worked the Wapping tunnel. Steam for the engines was supplied by four return-flue boilers, two per engine, set up in excavations on either side of the arch. The winding gear was supplied by William Fairbairn of Manchester.

'A Tourist' writing in 1831 left his vivid impression of arriving at Edge Hill:

> ... the grand entrance arch to Liverpool. This is a beautiful stuccoed structure in the Arabesque style of architecture, being surmounted by four embattlemented turrets, two of which project outward in the form of wings. The elevation of the arch from the railway is about forty feet, and its span about five and thirty ... An ornamental termination of the line was not, however, the sole design in its erection; in the interior of the building the two fixed engines, used as the impulsive force along the tunnels, busily ply their assigned task ...

> Passing underneath the arch we enter a noble area dug out of solid rock to a depth of forty feet below the natural surface of the ground. The plane of this area is perfectly level; and the sides and end are surmounted by massive brick walls, rising six feet above the summit of the excavation, crowned by embattlemented stone copings assimilating with the turrets of the Moorish arch. The entire admeasurement is about one hundred and fifty feet long, seventy feet wide, and forty-six feet high from the base to the battlements ...

The Grand Area of Edge Hill depicted by Bury in 1835. The twin chimneys became known as the 'Pillars of Hercules'. The blind southern tunnel entrance (only included for the sake of symmetry) was probably used as an engine shed. (Author's Collection)

> The *tout ensemble* of this grand entrance, as viewed from the interior, forms a spacious and beautifully proportioned parallelogram, and has an appearance worthy of the great work of which it is a prominent ornamental feature.

A number of openings cut into the solid rock can still be seen on both sides of the 'Grand Area': those on the south side are much truncated and many features were destroyed when the cutting was widened by 3 metres on that side in 1864. On the south side are two pairs of openings, much truncated. An archaeological survey in 1979 revealed that the eastern-most pair (immediately west of the site of the Moorish Arch) are 12.6 metres deep, 5.1 metres and 6.15 metres wide respectively and 3.8 metres tall. The two are linked about 1 metre in from the entrance by a smaller tunnel, which probably led to the engine house. They are clearly illustrated by Thomas Bury in two versions of his print of the 'Entrance of the Railway at Edge Hill'. The earliest, dated February 1831, shows the south engine chimney under construction and shows the brick lining to both of these openings. In the second version, dated 1835, the southern chimney is complete and smoking. Bury clearly shows the ends of a pair of 'Lancashire Boilers' in the arch of each of the openings. Confusingly, however, his 1831 view of the Moorish Arch, Bury, shows a siding with a turn-table

The overgrown and litter-strewn Grand Area at Edgehill in 2016; visible on the left (south) side are the two pairs of rock-carved openings for boilers to provide steam for the winding engines. On the right (north) side can be seen a corresponding pair of boiler houses. Thomas Bury shows the nearest pairs housing 'Lancashire Boilers' in 1835. Additional rock-carved openings on the north side for an additional boiler house, water tank and staff accommodation are masked by vegetation. (Author)

immediately in front of the westernmost openings, with a *Meteor*-type locomotive being turned and serviced. Perhaps these openings were used temporarily for the servicing of locomotives until the winding engine was installed.

Moving further west is a second pair of arched openings, which are not depicted by Bury, suggesting they were constructed after *c.* 1835. They are smaller than the first pair, being 4.3 metres wide and 3.25 metres high. The 1979 report concluded that they were probably the boiler houses for the southern winding engine, which contradicts the evidence from Bury's prints. The easternmost opening was converted to staff accommodation by the inserting of a brick wall in front. The large, round smoke tunnel leading off to the south chimney is still extent and open for much of its distance.

On the north side, the archaeology is better preserved; there are three openings cut into the rock. There are two openings immediately to the west of the site of the north winding engine house, which are depicted by Bury as being boiler houses: he clearly shows the ends of 'Lancashire Boilers' installed in both of them in 1835. To the west of them is a staircase cut into the rock face to provide staff access. The third, and westernmost, opening is not depicted by Bury. It was identified in 1979 as being a boiler house: 2.4 metres wide and 13 metres deep. Moving further west were rock-carved rooms for staff accommodation as shown on the prints by Thomas Bury.

Both chimneys are now demolished; over 100 feet high, they were built in a course of spiral brickwork, and finished to resemble massive Doric columns, with stone capitals and pediments. The northern chimney was finished by 1831; the second by 1835. The Moorish Arch and southern engine house were demolished in 1864.

The Tunnels

There were two tunnels constructed at the western end of the 'Grand Area' – the northern (and the smallest) led to Crown Street. The central tunnel led to the Wapping goods yard. And, for the sake of symmetry, a third blind tunnel portal was excavated on the south side. Bury (1835) shows it fitted with doors and a locomotive standing outside, suggesting that it was used as an engine shed. It was opened out in 1846, and again in 1864, to provide additional access to Crown Street.

The Wapping Tunnel was considered to be a 'wonder of the age' when finished in 1830 at a cost of £44,700. It was 1.26 miles long, with a falling gradient of 1:48. The double track tunnel was 22 feet wide and 16 feet high. 'Luggage trains' were run down under gravity into the yard and hauled by up using the winding engine. Work started on the tunnel in January 1827; John Foster was appointed as principal engineer in charge of the tunnel with a salary of £400 per annum. In August Joseph Locke was made responsible for the Liverpool or 'western' end of the railway, including the tunnels. Foster, however, was unwilling to serve under Locke. The directors, however, were unwilling to give total charge of the line to George Stephenson or his assistants and so, on 4 September, appointed Jesse Hartley as civil engineer and inspecting engineer. The route of the tunnel had already been marked out by Charles Vignoles in 1826 but, when work commenced, it was discovered by George Stephenson that the three pilot shafts (or 'eyes') were not quite in line. Stephenson reported to the directors in December 1826 and put the blame squarely on Vignoles, who subsequently admitted the mistake had been made during the 'poling out' while he had been absent. This led to a confrontation between the two men, and one which had been coming for some time. Stephenson was something of a micro-manager: 'he does not look on the concern with a liberal and expanded view; but considers it with a microscopic eye, magnifying the importance of derails ... pursuing a petty system of parsimony ...' Vignoles considered that the best way to make friends with Stephenson was to 'cry down all other engineers' and to give him 'sycophantic expressions of praise'. Vignoles resigned

The three tunnel mouths in 2016: the 1860s double-track tunnel to Crown Street, which necessitated the widening of the cutting by several metres, is on the left; the original 1830 double-track tunnel to Wapping goods depot is in the centre; and the single-track tunnel down to Crown Street station on the right. (Author)

Interior of the 1.26-mile-long Wapping Tunnel. Internally it was painted white and lit by gas lamps placed every 50 yards. The tunnel was open to public view from its completion in July 1829, and tickets were available at 'moderate cost'. The tunnel was double-track: goods trains were let down to Wapping by gravity and pulled up to Edge Hill on a 1:48 gradient by the winding engine. At the top, the train was marshalled and a locomotive attached. (Author's Collection)

on 2 February 1827, much to the satisfaction of Stephenson, as he now had sole charge of the line, having previously been able to get rid of the Rennies. In private, however, the directors expressed their regret to Vignoles that the 'queer temper of Mr Stephenson' had led to his departure.

The tunnel was the subject of frequent visitors; the directors were advertising tours in October 1829 for an 'extremely moderate' fee. 'A Tourist' in 1831 wrote,

> This is an immense excavation, twenty feet in width, and sixteen high, the sides of which rise perpendicularly for five feet, and are surmounted by a semi circular arch, with a radius of eleven feet. The interior is painted white, and illuminated by gas lights projecting from the centre of the arch ... the whole surface being whitened, prevents any idea of insecurity in the mind of the passenger ...

The Crown Street Tunnel was 290 yards long, with a rising gradient of 1:48. It was never large enough to admit locomotives being only 15 feet wide and 12 foot high. Like the Wapping tunnel, it was painted white internally and lit by gas.

It was only in the 1890s when locomotives were first used in the Wapping tunnel, and then in the Up direction only; trains heading toward Wapping were still controlled by gravity. To the east of Wapping, the tunnel was opened out to create a cutting and ventilation shafts were built to disperse the smoke from the locomotives, which began work in May 1896. At the same time two new tunnels were made, linking an enlarged Wapping goods station to Edge Hill. Diesel shunters were introduced in the 1930s, which made conditions in the tunnel more bearable for the locomotive crews. Wapping tunnel and the branch to Wapping goods station closed in November 1965.

Wapping

The main Liverpool 'goods station' was at Wapping, in an open area approximately 46 feet wide and 22 feet below ground level. The railway ran under a large, brick-built warehouse, 100 feet long and supported of the rails by cast-iron columns. The rail

> ... branches into four lines; and the rails are fixed upon moveable wooden circles to afford a facility in turning the wagons. The goods are hoisted from the wagons through hatchways made in the flooring of the warehouses above.

Wapping goods depot in Liverpool as depicted by Bury in 1831. The depot was described by Henry Booth as 'an open cutting, 22 feet deep and 46 feet wide, being space for four lines of Railway, with pillars between the lines to support the beams and flooring of the Company's warehouses, which are thrown across this excavation, and under which the wagons pass to be loaded or discharged through hatchways or trapdoors communicating with the stores above'. (Author's Collection)

Arched recesses were ordered to be dug into the walls of the cutting in November 1830 to store empty goods wagons, and sidings were laid between Wapping and Ironmonger Lane for the storage of wagons in 1833. Additional sheds were built towards Crosbie Street in 1831. As at Liverpool Road, accommodation was soon expanded; in summer 1831 the company provided a warehouse, shipping wharfs and a crane for the Bolton & Leigh Railway at Wapping at an annual charge of £150. A further shed and offices were built in 1838. Late in 1839 a steam engine was installed to work the numerous warehouse hoists and cranes at Wapping. Wapping goods station closed in 1965 and in 2015 is a light industrial area.

Crown Street

The Liverpool terminus of the Liverpool & Manchester was at Crown Street, as with Liverpool Road, then on the edge of the city. In fact, Crown Street was so far out of town that the streets were unpaved – including Crown Street itself until sometime after the railway opened. The company provided omnibuses for first-class passengers only from its

Built in a somewhat out-of-town location, the Railway Office Liverpool on Crown Street was a modest stone building (probably designed by John Foster), which sported what was probably the first overall station roof. (Author's Collection)

offices in Dale Street, which departed 20 minutes before the train. They operated on three different routes:

> Dale Street – Sir Thomas's Buildings – Williamson Square – Clayton Square – Ranelagh Street – Mount Pleasant – Oxford Street.
> Dale Street – North John Street – Lord Street – Church Street – Bold Street – Leece Street – Hope Street – Falkner Street.
> Dale Street – Manchester Street – Lime Street – London Road, Seymour Street – Russel Street – Clarence Street – Mount Plesant – Oxford Street.

They would 'pick up or set down at a point in the above-mentioned Routes, but ... the Company cannot engage to call for any Passenger at any particular place on the Route'. Nor could the company 'secure room in the omnibus after it has once set out'. Seats were on first-come, first-served basis.

The 'bus was free of charge for

> ... sixty-eight Passengers and their luggage (the said number, *first booked*, having the preference on their claiming it at the time of booking), and for the same number from Crown-Street to Dale-Street on the arrival of the Coaches from Manchester, a preference on the same terms being given to Passengers first booked at the Company's Coach-offices, Manchester.

During the Newton Race Week, 'during which it is impossible to ensure the desired accommodation', a 'conveyance to and from Crown-Street will be provided' for all first-class passengers. Each passenger was allowed up to 60 lbs of luggage *gratis* and 3 s per cwt thereafter. Passengers were not allowed to tip any of the porters, guards or coachmen (as had been the custom on the stage-coach); nor was smoking allowed, so as to prevent the 'annoyance' of other passengers.

James Scott Walker described Crown Street in 1830:

> ... the visitor finds himself in large yard of the Company ... A space on one side, is appropriated for coals, and on the other is a rang of coach-houses for the Rail-Way carriages. In front of the latter is a handsome building, intended as offices for the clerks of the Company, coach-offices and apartments for the reception and accommodation of passengers ...

The stone station building was restrained neoclassical, and it supported along the track side an overall roof – perhaps the world's first – which was used to shelter passengers, and also store trains of carriages when not in use. Locomotives did not work into Crown Street – they had already been detached at Edge Hill and trains ascended into the station, worked by endless rope that was driven by a stationary edge. They left under gravity, running down into Edge Hill controlled by a brakesman.

It was at Crown Street that the 'Grand Procession' of the opening day (15 September 1830) began: 'The persons to whom places were assigned ... [were] requested to assemble ... not later than half-past nine in the morning.'

Above: The site of Crown Street station today: closed to passengers in 1836, it became a coal yard, which in turn closed in 1972. Derelict for many years, it was cleared and became a popular park in the 1980s. (Author)

Left: Some of the old railway remains at Crown Street: a pile of old stone sleeper blocks provides a small clue as to the history of the park. (Author)

Above: Another reminder of the history of Crown Street Park, welcoming visitors to Crown Street and the 'western terminus of the world's first passenger railway'. (Author)

Right: The 1890s ventilator tunnel built to allow locomotive working – albeit in one direction only – through the extensive system of railway tunnels under Liverpool to the docks. One railwayman in the 1950s remembered: 'It was quite a frightening experience ... with its everlasting pall of smoke ... Under the bowels of Liverpool, we were never at any time able to catch a glimpse ... or even a pinprick of light'. (Author)

Gray's Yard

Alongside Crown Street, in Millfield Yard, were the workshops of William Gray; his son, John, was in charge of the carriage and wagon department. The 'Carriage Building Department' had been established by Thomas Clarke Wordsell (Chapter 2) in 1828, of a Quaker family of coachbuilders who settled in Liverpool from London.

Locomotives were repaired at Brickfield station (immediately east of the Moorish Arch), while heavy forgings, spring-making and boiler-making took place at Gray's Yard. Boiler-making only commenced on the Liverpool & Manchester in 1832 at the suggestion of John Melling (Chapter 2). Prior to that date, boiler work had been contracted out to local firms. In April 1832, the directors agreed to employ 'three boiler makers, instead of employing Foster & Griffin for that kind of work'. Four months later, the directors resolved to concentrate heavy repair in Liverpool with light repair and maintenance work being carried out by Fyfe at Manchester. Following this decision, the directors invested £1,000 in machine tools, including a hydraulic wheel press. On the closure of Crown Street station to passengers in 1836, the works were greatly expanded; Francis Wishaw lists Gray's Yard as being quite extensive:

> There is a smithy with thirty-six hearths, a spacious foundry, a boiler-maker's shop, wagon-building and repairing shop, besides considerable space for coal wagons ... there were not few than ninety men employed as smiths, boiler-makers, and spring-makers.

With the advent of the Grand Junction Railway in 1837, all repair facilities were to be concentrated at Edge Hill, under the superintendence of Melling; the new workshops were first on the south side of the line, but were extended to the north in 1838; in January 1839, the company purchased an additional 10,000 square yards for further extensions.

Lime Street

It became immediately apparent to the directors that Crown Street was 'too far removed' from the centre of Liverpool ever to function as that town's principal station; as early as 9 May 1831 a subcommittee recommended that a survey be made to bring the railway into the town itself. In June Stephenson produced a plan for bringing the line from Edge Hill (where a station would be built) through a tunnel to what would become Lime Street station. This plan was approved by a general meeting of the shareholders in September 1831 and the Empowering Act received Royal Assent on 23 May 1832. The new Lime Street station was opened in 1836 (still unfinished) at a cost of £6,123 of which £2,000 came from Liverpool Council. Lime Street was approached by a tunnel over a mile long; it was opened out into a cutting in the 1880s, allowing locomotives to work through to the station. Lime Street was enlarged again from 1842 to 1849 (for £30,000), again from 1865 to 1867 and from 1879 to 1880. The current Lime Street Hotel, designed by Quaker architect Alfred Waterhouse ARA was built in 1879. A new passenger station was opened at Edge Hill in 1836.

Planet at dusk, the last rays of sunlight gilding her brass work. (Ian Hardman Photography)

Crown Street closed to passengers in 1836 and became a coal depot; it closed 1972 and became derelict. It was laid out as a park in the 1980s and, other than the western portal of the 1860s tunnel (used by Merseyrail as a head shunt), nothing remains of Liverpool's first passenger railway station.

Afterword

Liverpool Road station closed on 8 September 1975, by which point it was becoming an increasingly dilapidated embarrassment. The local press had been ringing alarm bells over the state of the buildings for some time; the *Manchester Evening News* in March 1973 referred to it as 'history now crumbling on platform one', while a year later the *Manchester Guardian* described it as 'decaying and unkempt in a redevelopment area'. Questions had even been raised in parliament in 1972 over the 'tattiness of a monument to the greatest revolution in travel and communications'. In response, British Railways sought corporate sponsorship for the cost of repairs.

The buildings were surveyed by Greater Manchester Council in 1975. It was estimated it would take £1.2 million to restore and redevelop the site as a museum. During the following year, the council made urgent repairs to the buildings to make them weatherproof, the city council viewing the original 1830s buildings as the potential home for a railway museum. The Victorian Society made a strong effort throughout 1976 to motivate railway societies to encourage official bodies to save the site.

The site's saviour was the Liverpool Road Station Society, formed in January 1978 with the aims of 'securing the station's future for museum use and ensuring that Manchester celebrated its 150th anniversary in 1980 in an appropriate manner'. David Rhodes was chairman and Jane Kennedy, secretary. The society produced a comprehensive report detailing how the site could be restored and run as a trustee-led railway museum, which would also organise the 1980 celebrations. The site was purchased by Greater Manchester Council for the nominal sum of £1 in 1978; the 'shipping shed' was also purchased, together with an additional plot of land to serve as an exhibition hall and, after considerable pressure, the Greater Manchester Council also agreed to the cost of relaying the track for £30,000. Consolidation and restoration of the buildings began in June 1979 by consulting architects Thomas Worthington & Sons, and many features not thought to belong to the original 1830s station were cleared away. Track work was completed by December 1979. The freight office became an interpretation centre and museum space. The Greater Manchester Council designated the Castlefield area of Manchester, in which Liverpool Road station stands, as an 'outstanding conservation area' in 1980. The main-line connection at Liverpool Road meant it was used as one of the stabling points for the 'Rocket 150' celebrations of 1980 and many famous locomotives visited the site, including *Flying Scotsman*, *Sir Nigel Gresley* and *Lion*, the only surviving Liverpool & Manchester locomotive, which arrived from Wigan under her own steam. During summer 1980, an eight-week-long exhibition and festival was held at Liverpool Road, climaxing on 14 September when a celebratory train with historic locomotives and carriages ran from Liverpool to Manchester Liverpool Road. In more recent years, the main-line connection allowed visits by the Royal Train, headed by *Tornado* (2010), and *Oliver Cromwell* (2012).

Part of the site was earmarked as a new home for the North West Museum of Science and Industry (opened 1969), which had outgrown its former home on Grosvenor Street. The new museum opened, quite fittingly, on 15 September 1983 as the Greater Manchester Museum of Science and Industry.

If it had not been for the dedication of the volunteer-led Liverpool Road Station Society, it is likely that the Manchester end of the Liverpool & Manchester Railway would have met the same ignominious fate as that in Liverpool – abandonment and demolition. To them we owe a huge debt of gratitude.

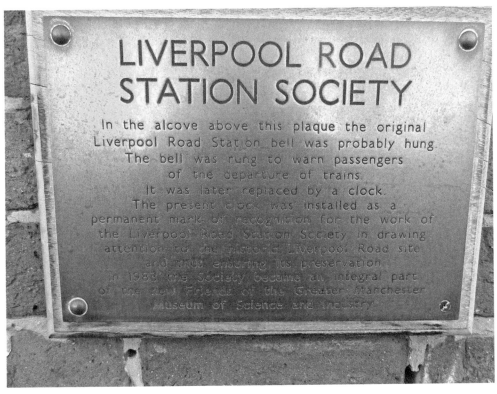

Commemorative plaque at Liverpool Road to mark the work of the Liverpool Road Station Society in preserving the world's first inter-city passenger railway station.

Select Bibliography

Contemporary newspapers and journals:

American Railroad Journal
Herapath's Railway Magazine
The Railway Magazine
Liverpool Chronicle
Liverpool General Advertiser
Liverpool Mercury
Manchester Courier
Manchester Guardian
Manchester Mercury
Manchester Times
The Engineer
The Mechanic's Magazine

Books and Pamphlets

Anon, *A History and Description of the Liverpool and Manchester Railway* (Liverpool: Thomas Taylor, 1832).

Anon, *Panorama of Manchester and Railway Companion* (Manchester: J. Everett, 1834).

'A Tourist', *The Railway Companion, Describing an Excursion on the Liverpool Line* (London: Effingham Wilson, 1833).

H. Booth, *An Account of the Liverpool and Manchester Railway ...* (Liverpool: Wales & Baines, 1830).

D. K. Clark, *Railway Machinery: A Treatise on the Mechanical Engineering of Railways* (London: Blackie & Son, 1855).

L. Herbert, *A Practical Treatise on Railroads* (London: Thomas Kelly, 1837).

Lieutenant P. Lecount, *A Practical Treatise on Railways* (Edinburgh: Adam & Charles Black, 1839).

T. Tredgold, *Explanation of the Machinery of Locomotive Engines* (London: John Weale, 1850).

J. S. Walker, *An Accurate Description of the Liverpool and Manchester Railway* (Liverpool: J. F. Cannell, 1830).

F. Wishaw, *The Railways of Great Britain Practically Described and Illustrated* (London: Simpkin, Marshall & Co., 1840).

Secondary Books and Pamphlets

'Anon', *One Hundred Years Ago. The early history of the Liverpool and Manchester Railway* (Manchester: Beyer, Peacock Ltd., 1930).

R. E. Carlson, *The Liverpool & Manchester Railway Project* (Newton Abbot: David & Charles, 1969).

C. F. Dendy Marshall, *Centenary History of the Liverpool and Manchester Railway* (London: Locomotive Publishing, 1930).

C. F. Dendy Marshall, *One Hundred Years of Railways* (London: London Midland & Scottish Railway Co., 1930).

T. J. Donaghy, *Liverpool & Manchester Railway Operations 1831-1845* (Newton Abbot: David & Charles, 1972).

R. S. Fitzgerald, *Liverpool Road Station, Manchester* (Manchester: Manchester University Press, 1980).

R. V. Holt, *The Unitarian Contribution to Social Progress in England* (London: Allen & Unwin, 1938).

C. Makepeace, ed., *Oldest in the World. The story of Liverpool Road Station*, Manchester (Manchester: Liverpool Road Railway Society, nd).

R. Watts, Gender, *Power and the Unitarians in England* (1760-1860) (London: Routledge, 2013).

R. B. Williams, *Accounting for Steam and Cotton* (New York: Garland, 1997).